Advance Praise for

# I Can See Clearly Now

Dr. DeLong's book is masterfully crafted, simply told, and relatable to all readers, with a powerful message on living life with purpose. This book is an absolute must read. Share with loved ones and buckle up book club readers! This book is for you!

—Alexandra Quinn, MSN, CRNP, BSN, Certified, Registered Nurse Practitioner

Heartfelt and inspiring while heartbreaking and healing, Peggy DeLong's book weaves through a time of loss, speaking her truth with courage and soul, reminding us all of the power to merge the past and the present in a powerful love story. This memoir is written to inspire and succeeds triumphantly.

—Mary-Michael Levitt, LPC, LMFT, DRCC

This book is recommended reading for anyone losing hope that a full life is possible after loss, difficulty, or tragedy. The author emerged from the darkness of grief to shine a light on this process for others. She teaches that it is possible to live in love and wholeness after the unthinkable has occurred.

—Megan McDowell, LPC, MSW, Founder, Heartworks Foundation

*I Can See Clearly Now* is a concise work of nonfiction that takes the reader on a harrowing, emotional journey through the death of loved ones. With heart-wrenching detail, raw honesty, passion, and humor, Peggy generously shares her remarkable story, giving hope to anyone who has loved and lost.

—Kristen Henderson, poet, author of *Drum Machine* and *Of My Maiden Smoking*

Peggy DeLong has written an inspiring memoir that will grab your heart and not let go until the final word. This book is a truly moving experience, one where you travel from profound loss to love and the gift of eternal life that never dies.

—Irene Weinberg, Author of *They Serve Bagels in Heaven: One Couple's Story of Love, Eternity and the Cosmic Importance of Everyday Life*; Creator and Host of the podcast, *Grief and Rebirth: Finding the Joy in Life*

This book of love and loss and the journey of recovery gave me such hope. In this book, DeLong shared how when life becomes overwhelming, following the path of hope and faith can lead to healing, change, and newfound love. The writing is gentle and comforting. As a reader, you feel as though Peggy is the girl next door, and you are there as a friend, helping her move through her story.

—Kim Albertson, M.Ed.

Peggy DeLong's story is a tale of devastating loss. Knowing her loved ones lived on in spirit, she is able to thrive in life again. Peggy's optimistic outlook and capacity for love is truly inspirational to those who have had to navigate through their own suffering and uncertainty about how they will ever be able to live and love again.

—Madeline Park, Chief Operating Officer of Red Fuse and Lean Six Sigma Master Black Belt

This is a lovely story with an inspiring outlook on love and life. By the end, the writer has come full circle, and the reader feels full of hope. This book will touch so many lives. Bravo!

—Suzanne Martin-Pillsbury, MS

Peggy's memoir is an authentic and revealing account of two devastating losses in the life of a young woman. In the end, *I Can See Clearly Now* is a story of love, patience, and resilience. This book will be a source of hope for anyone struggling to live when important others have died.

—Jenny Meyer Colman, MD, Psychiatrist, Bard and Marist Colleges

In her book and her life, Dr. Peggy DeLong proves that distance, time, best-laid plans, and even death are no match for love. Love and gratitude endure and will always find a way to brighten the darkest of hours with a wink of an eye or a cup of hazelnut coffee. This book is necessary reading for anyone who has experienced loss of any kind.

—Linda Moakler, author of "Paper Flowers," published by *The Mighty*

Peggy DeLong takes us on a visceral journey through deep loss and grief. What's marvelous about this story is that Peggy takes us through the process of healing, where we can find hope and love on the other side of those truly dark days.

—Carol Richmond, Holistic Health Coach

This is a heartbreaking story of a woman who goes through so much love and loss, yet she continues to live with hope and faith. This book will make you believe you can overcome anything.

—Carley Storm, Photographer and Video Producer

This is an incredibly moving story. I felt I was with Peggy every step of the way through her journey from grief to joy. I could feel her pain and also her happiness as she went through a most difficult period in her life to a bright, bright sunshiny day.

—Carol Doherty

I found beautiful lessons in the pages of Peggy DeLong's honest, raw, and heartfelt life and love story, *I Can See Clearly No*w. Peggy's powerful words reminded me to always value and be grateful for the precious relationships in my life.

—Tara Gilvar, CEO and Founder of B.I.G. (Believe, Inspire, Grow)

Peggy opens her big heart and shares her joy and devastation in equal measure. I particularly resonated with the love between mother and daughter in this book. Peggy's mom, Carol, is her bedrock . . . a consistent and vital part of Peggy's life story. I like to think that Carol's extraordinary mothering inspired Peggy in her relationship with her children, a connection infused with empathy and a belief that love will win.

—Julie Kahn

This author had me within the first few pages. I would award an A+ to this book and will suggest it to my family and friends so they can also enjoy this magical woman's journey!

—Cheryl Beneduce Bock,
President and Founder of Pedal for a Cure

On a scale from 1 to 10 of monumental reads, I would give *I Can See Clearly Now* an 11. Wow. I laughed. I cried several times. Peggy shines through with grace and composure, giving glimmers of what irrefutable hope looks like. Peggy's triumphal ending will inspire readers who have known or are in tragic situations.

—Kathleen Bandaruk, President,
Tastefully Inspired Digital Marketing Agency

# I Can See Clearly Now

A Memoir about Love, Grief, and Gratitude

# I Can See Clearly Now

## A Memoir about Love, Grief, and Gratitude

Dr. Peggy Doherty DeLong,
The Gratitude Psychologist

PEACOCK PROUD
P·R·E·S·S

Phoenix, Arizona

I Can See Clearly Now: A Memoir about Love, Grief, and Gratitude

Copyright © 2019 by Dr. Peggy Doherty DeLong

First Published in the USA in 2019 by Peacock Proud Press, Phoenix, Arizona

ISBN 978-1-7322427-2-2 paperback

ISBN 978-1-7322427-3-9 eBook

LCCN: 2019937400

All rights reserved. No part of this publication may be reproduced, stored in or introduced into a retrieval system, or transmitted, in any form, or by any means (electronic, mechanical, photocopying, recording or otherwise) without the prior written permission of the publisher. This book is sold subject to the condition that it shall not, by way of trade or otherwise, be lent, resold, hired out, or otherwise circulated without the publisher's prior consent in any form of binding or cover other than that in which it is published and without a similar condition, including this condition being imposed on the subsequent purchaser.

**Editors**: Laura L. Bush, PhD, PeacockProud.com

Wendy Ledger, VoType.com

Lorraine Ash, LorraineAsh.com

Krissa Lagos of Warner Coaching, BrookeWarner.com

**Cover and Interior Layout**: Melinda Tipton Martin, MartinPublishingServices.com

**Portrait Photographer**: Maryanne Teng Hogarth, MaryanneTengHogarth.com

**DISCLAIMER:**

This is a work of nonfiction. The information is of a general nature to help readers know and understand more about the life of the author, Dr. Peggy Doherty DeLong. Readers of this publication agree that Dr. Peggy Doherty DeLong will not be held responsible or liable for damages that may be alleged or resulting directly or indirectly from their use of this publication. All external links are provided as a resource only and are not guaranteed to remain active for any length of time. The author cannot be held accountable for the information provided by, or actions resulting from accessing these resources.

For my mother, Carol Doherty. For showering me with an abundance of unconditional love. For making me believe I could do anything I set my mind to. For your gentle, quiet, humble strength. For always being my rock, even during your own time of grief. For showing me courage and bravery in living and loving after loss. For loving my husband as your own son and for caring for my children as your own. For always demonstrating for me what it means to be a caring, loving, giving human being. Because of you, I am who I am. I love you, Mom.

# Contents

Acknowledgments ................................................................... xiii

Foreword ............................................................................... xvii

Prologue ................................................................................. xix

Sister Golden Hair ..................................................................... 1

The Last Summer ..................................................................... 33

Death's Door ........................................................................... 65

The Chairlift ............................................................................ 85

Ring of Power ........................................................................ 105

Return of Passion .................................................................. 115

The Choice ............................................................................ 139

Epilogue ................................................................................ 155

About the Author .................................................................. 159

# Acknowledgments

*I* would like to thank the people who not only influenced the creation of this book, but who played a role in my life and healing process.

To my childhood girlfriends, for all your love and laughter over the years. We are blessed to have our lifelong friendships. Thank you for seeing me through my darkest time. Thank you for celebrating with me when I found love again.

To Megan McDowell, for your support through our frequent walks, which were instrumental in my healing.

To my former therapist, Judith Springer, PsyD. I simply do not know how I would have processed my grief without your understanding and comfort.

To the former bereavement group facilitator at St. Patrick's Church in Chatham, Pam Koch, for providing a safe and sacred place for those who were grieving.

To all of my former coworkers at the Therapeutic Learning Center at Newark Beth Israel Medical Center. I cannot imagine working at a more supportive, caring place when I needed it the most.

To all my Pocono friends for distracting me from my grief to enjoy the healing power of the mountains and the healing power of your friendship. A special thanks to Helen for being my silly partner in crime.

To my fellow doctoral students at Pace University, who were gentle and understanding that I was still grieving when our rigorous program started.

To Mary-Michael Levitt, for introducing me to my first editor, Lorraine Ash.

To Lorraine Ash, for your magic of organizing and transforming my chopping journal into an outline and chapters, and for helping me believe that this was a story that needed to be told.

To Brooke Warner of She Writes Press and Warner Coaching, for being interested in my story and connecting me with Krissa Lagos.

To my second editor, Krissa Lagos of Warner Coaching, for helping me dig deep and provide the sensory details and dialogue to help my story come to life.

To Susana Fonticoba, master connector, for connecting me with Laura Bush, PhD, and Peacock Proud Press.

To my editor Wendy Ledger, of VoType, for thoughtful and meticulous editing.

To Laura Bush of Peacock Proud Press, for your interest in my story from the beginning, unquestionable confidence that you could bring my book to publication, and your support every step of the way.

To the amazing women of Believe, Inspire, Grow (my tribe), for your support, encouragement, and inspiration. You helped me find my voice, and I have not stopped writing and speaking since!

To my sister, Debbie, and brothers, Brian and David, for all our wonderful childhood memories, for loving Scott as you did, and for welcoming John.

To my sister, Debbie, and brother-in-law, Don, for having me tag along on so many Pocono adventures the first eighteen months after Scott's passing.

To Ed Pittenger, for making my mother so happy.

To Scott's parents, Tom and Pat, for raising Scott to be the kind, generous, thoughtful, and loving man that he was. To Scott's parents and his sisters, Gretchen and Jill, for welcoming me in to your family. Thank you for honoring my relationship with Scott during his illness and after he passed.

To my late fiancé, Scott Unger, for the privilege of being by your side during your journey, and for teaching me important life lessons along the way. For teaching me that humor can make the darkness more tolerable. For teaching me to trust that there is more to this life than we know. For teaching me the healing power of gratitude, and to be grateful for the smallest, seemingly insignificant things. For teaching me the power of faith, hope, and love. For loving me fiercely and bravely, even when you knew you might not be around to share the rest of your life with me. For showing me in your own special way that you are still with me, and that you are happy for me and proud of the life I have created.

To my late father, Bill Doherty, MD, for everything. For your goofiness, child-like spirit, and sensitivity. For welcoming all my friends into our home. For cultivating my interest in mental health. For showing me the true meaning of family and fatherhood. For teaching me not to be afraid to feel and show emotion. For spending time with me skiing, biking, and hiking. For fostering my love of the outdoors, especially the mountains. For loving Scott like a son. For racing him on your mountain bike. For sledding with him down Stone Fence Road. For every minute you spent with him at the hospital. For being my rock after he passed. For giving me hope and making me believe that I would one day find love again. For wearing that silly clown wig so that I would know with certainty that you met and spoke with John.

For my three beautiful children, Caroline, Morgan, and Jamieson, for giving me the most important reason to be my best self every single day. You fill my heart with love, pride, and joy.

For my husband, John, my hero. For your bravery and courage in asking a young widow out on a date. For your compassion to be with someone whose heart had been hurt. For your depth to have conversations about love and profound loss, and the fear of loss. For your self-confidence to know you could make me happy. For your love and for creating this beautiful family and life with me.

# Foreword

In this heart-finding memoir, Peggy chronicles her relationship with her fiancé, Scott, and their quick segue to an exhaustive seven-month battle with cancer, punctuated by another unexpected loss of a family member. Peggy captures every surprise of her days with Scott—beautiful and horrifying, together and apart, alone and with family and friends—and your heart rises and falls along with them, this young couple on the brink of a future together that becomes painfully derailed.

One of the great surprises of this book is the newness/freshness of the writing, which belies the nearly-twenty-five-year-old journey that makes up this memoir. Every detail—from the giddiness and sweet gestures of new love to the crushing weight of a fateful day's discovery—reads like a recent memory. Peggy's emotions are so clear and familiar that you'll be tempted to stay up all night to read it—like a "for your eyes only" letter from an old friend deserving a thoughtful response in the morning.

This is the real deal: we see that the oft-chronicled Bermuda Triangle of love, life, and loss is not always a story about courage and understanding and hope, but instead, a rollercoaster of blurred days, often smothered in anger, disbelief, and despair. Through it all, Peggy shows unexpected honesty with herself and with us—the raw impatience, the need to feel supported and consoled, even self-pity. The stalled faith is so real and relatable, we breathe a collective sigh of relief to know it's OK to be human and hurting.

Even after twenty-five years, Peggy's story does not end with getting *over* the pain of loss and erasing the past. Rather, the "healing path" can and should, perhaps, be one of remembrance, one that stays with you and winds through your life, with all its twists and turns. Over time, some memories stay clearer than others, with some dark clouds and others bright stars. The ability to keep remembering and acknowledging all that makes up who we are is something to be grateful for, something we can share with those we love and come to love, who we open our hearts to while we keep on living. This may explain why we close our eyes when we try to remember something kept close to our heart. Often, with our eyes closed, we see life most clearly.

—Elizabeth Ketterson, JD, Estate Administration Attorney

# Prologue

## February 27, 1994

When Scott, my fiancé, got out of bed, I was expecting another luscious, lazy Sunday with the love of my life. But life took another turn.

"Peggy, can you come in here, please, and take a look at this?" he yelled from the bathroom in our apartment. Curious, I stepped into the tiny space next to the vintage claw-foot tub that dominated the room.

He was gazing at his neck in the mirror. I turned his body toward the light flowing into the Victorian floor-to-ceiling window. As soon as I saw the lump on the side of his neck, just below his ear, I felt a pit in my stomach. The flesh-colored lump was the shape and size of a quarter and stuck out like a rolling hill—so high that, from the angle at which I was standing, it appeared to cast a shadow.

It felt hard and solid. I wanted to wipe the feeling away from my fingertips, but the sensation would not go away, even after I removed my hand. I had kissed that neck the night before. Why hadn't I noticed it? How did I not feel it under my lips?

"Get that checked out as soon as possible, honey," I said.

Quickly, I left the bathroom and went to the bedroom where he could not see me. I stared out the window overlooking the parking lot and quietly cried. I had a feeling, a premonition, that this was something terrible, and that our lives were about to suddenly change. In an instant, my mind wandered and contemplated the very worst. I imagined my future self, looking out this window after his death. I felt so alone. I felt so sad. I had no idea what this lump was, but I could not shake the feeling that I would be living my life without him. We'd only just begun. How would I live without my love?

# Sister Golden Hair

### Summary 1992

After I finished my master's program in clinical psychology at Fairleigh Dickinson University, I was biding time. I'd decided to start my life in Colorado but, for the time being, I was bored in Bernardsville, New Jersey, my beautiful but sleepy hometown. There was nothing for a single twentysomething to do there. But the skiing out west was great. Plus, my brother David already was living in Vail, and my college roommate Jennifer was living near Boulder. My sweet old roommate was looking at apartments for me. Even though she was married with a baby, she was eager for me to come out and join her.

In the meantime, I spent most of my weekends biking, boating, hanging out, and partying with my ski-and-bike buddies in the Pocono Mountains of Pennsylvania. I was itching to start my life and begin my career, though, and to fall in love with someone. When I was not in the Poconos on weekends, I was spending time with an old high-school crush.

I had casually dated Chris the year before during the summer of 1991, going to parties and, occasionally, dinner or drinks. The exciting part was that he got me out of my boring town. I met fresh new faces. One was his best friend, Scott. When I went to parties with Chris in his hometown of Chatham, I spent more time with Scott than Chris.

Although Chris and Scott were best buddies, I learned from one of their friends that there was always some subtle rivalry going on between them. So I wasn't surprised when Scott purposefully flirted with me in front of Chris. I know now that their competitive nature pushed each other to be the best that they could be. When Chris and I decided on friendship rather than romance, I continued to attend the parties. Why not? Chris's friends had become my friends, and he said I was always welcome.

During that summer of 1991, Scott was attentive and funny. On one occasion, we were hopping from one party to another. As I didn't know the town well or where I was going, Scott quickly jumped into the passenger seat of my car.

"I want to make sure you get there," he said, with a wink and a smile. *Is this a safety concern, or does he want me there?* When it was time for me to leave the second party, I could not get Chris's attention above the crowd and noise. Even though we were no longer dating, I didn't want him to worry about me if he could not find me. When Scott saw me struggling to get Chris's attention, he said he would take care of it. Within two minutes, Chris was standing in front of me. After I said goodbye to Chris, I asked Scott what he did to get him there.

"I told him you fell off the balcony," he replied. I thought to myself, *This kid is half adorable, half nuts!* I could not believe that he would go to such extreme measures to capture Chris's attention. I thought he was crazy! At the same time, I found him so endearing that he would go to this extreme in order to help me.

A week later, I stopped by Chris's apartment on my way home from a late-night class I was taking to prepare for my doctoral program entrance exam. Due to the demands of graduate school, I knew my schedule soon wouldn't allow for much of a social life. After five minutes, Scott showed up. He asked me to go on a bike ride with him the next day. I was leaving for a vacation with my family in two days, so we made plans to go cycling before I left.

Even though I hardly knew Scott, I felt comfortable around him. I felt special *to* him. When I arrived at his house on North Hillside Avenue for the bike ride, his mother answered the door. I told myself not to be nervous, and that we were just friends going for a bike ride. I didn't believe what I was telling myself. We started out with him leading the way, pedaling in front of me, because I had no idea where he was taking me. We rode down his street, a sidewalk-lined road, passing one quaint old Colonial home after the other. He told me who lived in each house. He'd grown up on that street and seemed proud of it.

"This is my buddy Charlie's house. And this is my buddy Nick's house. They've both lived here forever, like me, and they've been my friends forever," he said. I thought about all of the fun he must have had with his boyhood friends living just a few houses away on this peaceful street. Maybe they had got into some mischief as well. I also thought that it was so sweet that he was not afraid to show how much his friends meant to him. My thoughts were interrupted when he quickly added, "They like you." *He talked to them about me?* Butterflies started to do a little dance in my stomach. But instead of feeling nervous, I felt excited, energized. He confessed that he told them that he invited me for a bike ride, and that they both said I was a "nice girl."

Scott did not give me time to respond, as he kept on talking and telling me who lived in each house. "This is Mrs. McKelvey's house. I remember she used to love watching me ride my bike down the street when I was a little boy." Then for a moment, his smile disappeared, and his voice lowered as he told me about the little boy who was paralyzed from a diving accident. He seemed saddened by this, and my interest increased in this handsome man as he further revealed his capacity to feel. On just this short stretch of road, I learned that he cared about people, and that his friendships meant so much to him.

At the end of his street we turned left, pedaled onto Weston Avenue, and made a right onto Center Street, leaving his quiet neighborhood behind and riding on a busy road for a short stretch. Soon we turned right onto Yale Street and then took another left, putting us back onto North Hillside and crossing over Princeton and Harvard streets. The roads seemed aptly named. The residents must have graduated from prestigious colleges and had great jobs to be able to afford the lovely homes.

When we arrived at the end of North Hillside, we came upon a metal gate and took a break.

"You have a beautiful smile," he told me. "You must be happy. You've been smiling the whole ride." I didn't realize I was smiling, but based on how I was feeling, I know I must have been.

"How would you know? I was behind you. Do you have eyes on the back of your head?" I joked.

"Nope. Your smile is so big, I can see it in my bike mirror." I looked at the mirror attached to the left side of his handlebars and smiled even wider. I was not the least bit embarrassed to show how much fun I was having with him.

Beyond the metal gate was the unfinished Route 24, a small stretch of roadway that was soon to become a major highway connecting Interstate Route 287 in Morris County with Route 78 in Union County. Back then, it was just plain black asphalt—beautiful, new, smooth, empty. I'd never been on anything like it. We squeezed through the fence to get onto the forbidden blackness, which I'm sure was illegal, but that made it even more exciting. We stopped at the very top of what was to become the entrance ramp. Standing and straddling our bikes at such a high elevation, we took in views of Madison and Chatham and, beyond them, the taller buildings of Summit. The skyscrapers of New York City were a faint silhouette in the distance.

I was thrilled to see the macadam stretched in front of us, even though I usually preferred the bumps and jolts of mountain biking over rocks and roots in the deep woods. On that pristine smoothness we'd pick up speed going down the hill. I loved going fast, but my fear of hitting a bump and falling typically prevented me from going as fast as I would like on roads. In second grade I'd fallen off my bike and ended up with a mouthful of gravel and a fat lip so big that I required plastic surgery when my mouth fully formed. But that day, with Scott, I felt free to go as fast as I wanted.

"Let's race down the entrance ramp!" Scott said. I pedaled with all my might to keep up with him. I flew so fast that I was sure that my feet were going to slip out of the grips on my pedals. When Scott stopped pedaling and began coasting, I was relieved. I caught my breath as I caught up with him. We pedaled for five miles, side by side and slower so we could talk to each other and look at each other. He asked about the scar on my knee, which was still pink, raised, and bumpy from surgery a year earlier.

"I had ACL reconstruction," I explained. "Totally blew out my ACL at Sugarbush on my last day of skiing in college. Trying to impress a boy."

"Did it work?"

"Not so much. We just got off the chairlift to take our first run, and I fell making my very first turn. I didn't have enough speed for the binding to release, so instead, I tore the ligament to shreds."

"Ouch," Scott replied. "That sounds pretty painful. But the scar is sexy. I'm impressed."

"That's exactly what my friend Kristen said!" I replied. "I told her my scar was ugly. She said no, that guys will look at that and think, *"Now there's a girl with total balls!"*

"Your friend Kristen is right."

Scott wore a bright shirt with orange, yellow, green, and blue wide and bold horizontal stripes. The shirt fit him snugly, showing the contours of his chest muscles. The sleeves were short enough to reveal his biceps. His short blond hair sparkled in the sun's rays. I was drawn to the charming twinkle in his eye when he looked at me. I found myself just wanting to look at him.

But I also was concerned that if we did not pay attention, we were going to miss the gate and not be able to get off the highway. Scott, however, seemed free of worry. He was familiar with all the backyards and probably could have told me who lived in each house. He knew exactly where to get off the fresh asphalt and re-enter the neighborhood.

Once we were back on suburban streets, I rode in front because I knew the way. And guess what I saw in my bike mirror? His big, bright smile. When he caught me looking, he gave an exaggerated wink. By the time we arrived back at his parents' house, I felt as though something had changed between us, and I felt giddy. I wondered if he felt it too. Scott loaded my bike onto my rack for me. I was so used to doing that myself, it felt wonderful to instead have this strong man do it for me.

Then I didn't hear from him for a year.

In August 1992, in the midst of my plans to move to Colorado, Chris called me. I hadn't heard from him in a year, either. We made a dinner date. A half hour later, Scott called.

"I heard the lyrics to an America song, and they made me think of you," he told me.

"Which one?" I asked. So he sang.

He sang the opening lines to "Sister Golden Hair," then paused. "How about we go out?" *Was this the same old rivalry?*

"I already have plans with Chris tonight," I said.

"Great," he replied, not accepting defeat. "I'll meet up with both of you. Where are you going?" So all three of us met at Argyle's, a bar for twentysomethings in Morristown. I spent most of the night talking to Scott.

The next day, Scott called again and asked me out to dinner. I was surprised since he knew I was moving to Colorado in a few weeks. *Maybe that makes it safe*, I thought. When he arrived to take me to the Black Horse Inn, I walked him down to the pool to meet my father, who was swimming and reading the paper after a day of work. They were at ease with each other. It was almost like they already were friends. Dad didn't give Scott that slightly threatening eye most fathers give. He didn't say, "Take care of my daughter, and don't you dare hurt her." My father was not the type of man who would say those things. In this situation, I also believe he knew that I would be cared for.

Scott and I went to the Black Horse Inn and talked for three hours straight. I didn't want the night to end. Although it was only our first date, he asked me to come to his nephew's christening that weekend. I was flattered that he asked me to accompany him to such an intimate family event. I had to decline. I was moving in two weeks, and my time left at home with my family was limited. I had already planned on spending the day with my parents.

"It's a shame you're moving," he said. "Before you go, I want you to see my house in Blairstown and go biking again." We walked back to his red Toyota Celica in the parking lot. Its headlamps were covered when not in use.

"Look at that," he said. "My car is winking at you." One of the covers was stuck open, revealing a round glass lamp. It really looked like the car was winking. I thought that this was so cute, as his car matched his charming personality. It seemed so fitting that he would have a winking car!

Although we had a wonderful time, we didn't have plans for another date, as I had turned down his invitation to go to his nephew's christening. Not getting together again seemed to make more sense to me. Why spend time, energy, and money on a girl who'd be gone in two weeks?

To my surprise, Scott called two days later. He asked what I would like to do. I told him to call me back around 5 o'clock when I'd be back from taking a long bike ride with my parents. Promptly at 5:00 p.m., he called. That night we drove to his house in Blairstown, about fifty minutes from my parents' place. We sat on his wooden deck and talked more.

We talked about his car accident. While he was a student at the County College of Morris, he was coming home from a party one night and fell asleep at the wheel. Although I didn't ask, he assured me he had not been drinking and that the medical records proved it. I found it endearing that he cared about what I thought about him, as if I would have judged him if he'd been drinking.

He was in a coma for three weeks, he told me, and then matter-of-factly recounted how family and friends kept vigil at his bedside. His mother created a schedule so there was always someone with him. No one knew if he would live or die.

Scott did not complain once as he described what he had gone through during his rehabilitation—first inpatient, then outpatient. During that time, he wondered if his legs would ever allow him to play hockey or soccer again, or if they would remain confused and weak. He'd been a star hockey player but had to relearn how to walk and talk—and that was just the physical part. The mental, emotional, and psychological effects of rehabilitation seemed to have taken even more of a toll on him. He had to learn to control his emotions, make lists to cope with his memory problems, and compartmentalize everything in his life so it all made sense to him.

"How did you get through that time of your life? Weren't you scared?" I asked.

"Peggy, there's no 'I' in T-E-A-M," he said. "I got through it with the help of my team—my family, my friends, the doctors, the physical therapists. They were my team." *He's so humble. He's not even taking credit for what he's overcome.*

Scott said he was then determined to earn a college degree. He didn't have his "team" at college. There, it was all him, only him. He was accepted into a program at Northeastern University where his cognitive challenges and new learning differences could be addressed. Earning a bachelor's degree is no easy feat, but Scott was talking about it like it was no big deal after he'd just spent nearly two years retraining his mind and body. I listened quietly.

"I can't believe all that you have been through," I said. He smiled.

"No biggie." Inwardly, I wept for the young man I did not know. Instead of seeing him as frail or damaged, I saw his strength. I knew I would be safe and protected with him. Then he topped it all off by telling me that he was struck by lightning.

"What?"

"Yes," he said, almost proudly. "When I was a student at Northeastern, I was watching a Harvard rugby game. It was raining, so I was holding an umbrella. All of a sudden, there was a huge boom. The lightning struck my umbrella. I could feel it go through me, and I fell to the ground."

"Were you OK? Did you need to go to the hospital?"

"No, it wasn't a big deal. I was just confused for a minute. I couldn't figure out what had happened to me until the people standing on either side of me told me. They saw it and heard it, but they didn't feel it like I did. It must have been serious because then the game was called off."

"I can't believe that happened to you. You survive a horrific car accident, and then you survive being struck by lightning! You must have nine lives, like a cat," I joked, wondering how many people are struck by lightning and survive. He was proving himself to be one special, interesting man.

As I held a cold beer bottle, my hand got wet from the condensation. When I placed the bottle on the rotting wooden picnic table on his deck, it made a ring of water around the base that seeped into the wood. I didn't mind the roughness of the bench under my thighs or the prickly feeling under my forearm when I reached for my drink. Being around him, I felt an increased appreciation for each moment. With this appreciation, I found that my senses were heightened, simply by being around him. I was feeling a kind of enjoyment I'd never quite felt before. I found my eyes drawn not only to his handsome face, but to his muscular thighs. His shorts were just above his knee so I could see the contour of his quadriceps.

The house was on a hillside, with the deck overlooking tall trees in the woods. The sun was setting, and the last light of the day shining through the leaves created a glow on his face. The sky was filled with orange, pink, and purple hues. As the sun went down, the fireflies came out and lit up the darkness here and there. Then came the music of crickets. When I was little, I called them "back-to-school crickets" because they were a reminder of summer's end. I felt wonderful but also sad, knowing I'd soon be leaving Scott in two weeks.

He often complimented me, calling me a "knockout" and "a natural beauty." I wondered if he could sense that I felt the same way about him. It was as if each word he uttered made him more attractive to me, more handsome, more sexy—the twinkle in his eye, the way he winked at me, his strong hands, his broad shoulders. My heart beat faster.

"As soon as I heard 'Sister Golden Hair' on the radio, I couldn't get you out of my mind," he said. "I remembered your golden hair and smile from our bike ride. I had to call you." He added that he was kicking himself that he hadn't called earlier in the summer. "If I had, maybe you wouldn't be moving."

We kept talking, and my attraction grew stronger. It was as if he read my mind that I wanted to be close to him as he inched closer to me on the bench. Our thighs touched. My heart raced. So confidently, he leaned over and placed his hand on my cheek, gently turning my face toward him, and kissed me.

He kissed me! He stroked my hair and back. It felt so good to be with him, to be touched by him. Our first kiss was long, passionate, and delicious. When we stopped, he put his arms around me and lifted my legs over his so that I was practically sitting in his lap. He touched the scar on my knee, the same scar that had impressed him a year ago during our bike ride. Some parts of it were still numb, while others were extremely sensitive to touch. Gently and slowly, Scott ran his finger along the entire length of the scar. I felt the sensation where his finger met my skin and throughout my body. His big, strong arms and chest pressed against me. To my surprise, he kept one arm wrapped around my back, then circled his other arm under the crease of my knees, lifted me up, and carried me to his bedroom. Once we got there, he placed me gently down on the ground, and I stood up. We had to break the romantic momentum to transform his multi-colored futon from a couch to a bed.

Before lying on the futon, he put on the Allman Brothers album, "Eat a Peach." The music was passionate and sweet, matching our kissing and touching. All the feelings that were building up inside me since that bike ride finally came out. I'd been holding back, suppressing my feelings for him, because I knew I'd be leaving. I'd been so afraid of getting hurt. But once we were together, all of my worries disappeared. It felt so right.

We talked, we kissed, we laughed, we hugged. I felt his muscles right under my fingertips. After kissing, we often just looked at each other and smiled. At other times, we lay next to each other and looked up at the ceiling, holding hands and listening to the music. At two o'clock in the morning, I turned toward him. He let go of my hand and slipped his arm under my shoulder and onto my back. Gently, he lifted my head up onto his shoulder. I fell asleep there with his arms wrapped around me. When I woke up at 7:00 a.m., his arms were still around me, as if we had not moved all night, remaining as close to each other's bodies as possible. He was already awake and gazing at me. He smiled. A twinkle lit his eyes.

Once we were up, we decided to get breakfast at the Blairstown Diner. We drove in his Celica to the diner, which was only a mile or two down the road from his house. From the outside, it looked like one of those old-fashioned diners, and I felt like I was stepping back in time. The whole experience felt surreal. We sat in a booth. The kind waitress seemed to sense our giddiness, our happiness at being together. She smiled and seemed particularly excited to take our order. Scott suggested I get a blueberry muffin. The waitress asked if I wanted mine toasted. I'd never had a toasted muffin, but I said, "Sure." The first buttery bite melted in my mouth.

After breakfast, Scott drove me back to his house. I wanted to be with him, but I knew my parents wanted to be with me, too, because I was leaving soon. We kissed goodbye in the driveway. I was afraid that if I went inside, I'd never want to leave.

The next day, Scott called and asked me to come over again. I had so much free time because I'd already finished my last day of work and was just packing and getting things ready to move in thirteen days. I'd been working at an insurance agency on winter breaks and summers right through my college years and first master's degree. The company had even thrown me a goodbye party.

I drove a half hour on the highway to Blairstown, then pulled off onto a winding country road. I turned onto a side road and drove up the steep hill to Scott's white, modern bi-level house, tucked among trees deep in the woods. I felt comfortable pulling in the driveway, grabbing my overnight bag, and walking in.

Scott seemed happy that my intention was to stay. He made me dinner: we enjoyed pasta and beer on the deck. We spent time with his roommates—a young couple and two toddlers. They seemed happy for us. We excused ourselves and went to Scott's bedroom. That night felt even more loving and intimate. As we lay in bed, he propped up his head on one elbow and regarded me. He looked into my eyes and sang "Nothing Tonight," by the band Trout Fishing in America, changing the lyrics to "I'm singin' my songs about Peggy tonight." Tears of joy and sadness rolled down my cheeks. *Why did I have to wait so long for him to come into my life? Why did he have to come along now when I'm moving?*

A few days later on a warm summer evening, we went to an Allman Brothers concert at Brendan Byrne Arena in East Rutherford. We arrived early to enjoy sandwiches and drinks in the parking lot before heading into the open amphitheater. On our way in, I had to go to the bathroom badly. The line for the portable toilets was really long—so long that I was still waiting when the band started playing the first song. Scott was so thrilled to hear those familiar musical notes that his knees nearly buckled in excitement. But he stayed in line with me, hugging me from behind the whole time. Finally, we walked to our seats. All night, he had his hand on my knee or an arm wrapped around me. When the Allman Brothers sang "Blue Sky," he said the words were written for me. He sang the lyrics along with the band, looking at me and smiling with that adorable twinkle in his eye. I was so incredibly happy.

Two days later, we spent the night at his family home. Scott's parents were away and needed someone to take care of their dog. We made dinner and talked about how we could possibly have a future together when I was moving in a week. My roommate from college called to tell me she'd found an apartment for me and offered to sign the lease on my behalf the next day.

"No," I found myself telling her. "I've had a change of plans." I slowly walked out of the room for some privacy. Scott didn't know about my decision yet. How could he? I didn't even know myself until the words were coming out of my mouth!

"What?" Jennifer asked. "What's going on?"

"Instead of moving to Colorado," I said, "I'm just going to be a ski bum there for the winter." I was torn. I felt a need to go out west, something I'd always wanted to do. Yet I wanted to be with Scott. I felt a promise for our future. But I knew I'd regret it if I never took the time for myself.

"I met someone," I quietly told her. "I mean I *really* met someone. And he's here in New Jersey. I know it sounds crazy, but I can't see myself living without him. I have to come out west, but I also know I have to come back to him."

Jennifer was very happy for me. I was a bridesmaid in her wedding two years earlier, and I knew she wanted that same happiness with a partner for me. "I understand. And I can't wait to meet him!" She added, "I'm happy for you." I could hear her tears in her words.

I hung up the phone and walked back into the room where Scott was relaxing and watching television. "What's going on?" he asked. "You've got tears in your eyes."

I blurted out, "I'm not going to live in Colorado. I mean, I'm going to live there for a little bit, but then I'm coming home. I'm coming back home to you. I changed my plans."

Scott was in shock when I told him—a good, relieved kind of shock. We walked the dog on the sidewalks lining his parents' quiet Chatham street, enjoying the night, mostly in silence.

"In a few years, I can see us married, walking our own dog through Chatham," he said. *Did he just say "married"?* My heart fluttered. I was so shocked that I couldn't say a word. I just looked at him and smiled. Then I was afraid that if I said anything, he would take it back. I just wanted to let my mind wander and think about us, married, walking our dog at night after dinner.

❄ ❄ ❄

A few days later, my parents hosted a goodbye party for me. My family and all my closest friends were there with their boyfriends. They all loved Scott. At the end of the evening, Scott and I drove my Aunt Ruth home. She didn't drive at night, so my father always drove her the half hour to her home in Madison. I was proud of Scott when he offered to take her. On the way back, he and I were able to spend some time alone. That's the first time it hit me hard that I was leaving the man of my dreams in two days. *How can it possibly be that I started dating him two weeks ago and now cannot imagine life without him?* But he and I also knew I had to experience skiing out west. We dealt with our feelings by talking about our plans when I returned.

"Where would you like to live?" he asked. I replied that I would prefer to remain in the suburbs.

"I could never see myself living in Hoboken or New York City," I said, but it was almost as if my answer didn't matter because he was adamant that he wanted to live in Chatham.

"Maybe we can get an apartment in Chatham to start," he said. "Then we can get jobs, save some money, and buy a house here. But it will have to be small." As we drove through Madison, a community similar to Chatham, he pointed to a small Colonial. "Kind of like this house. Do you like this house? You know these houses are really expensive."

"A small house is fine with me. And yeah, I can definitely see myself living in Chatham," I assured him.

"How many kids do you want?" he asked. We agreed we'd like more than two children since we both grew up in families with more than one sibling.

"But what if we have three girls?" I joked. I knew he'd be happy with daughters, but that he also would like to have a boy.

"Then I guess we'll have to have four," he said. "Or five!"

The next night, Tuesday, September 9, 1992, was the eve of my departure. We kept busy to avoid the emotional pain of the pending separation—going for long hikes, walking his dog, helping my father in the yard, and spending time with my friends, who were fast becoming his friends.

Finally, we went to the classy Bernards Inn, where my dear friend Jody was singing and playing the piano. During dinner, I got hives for the first time in my life. My forearms were covered in red blotches. My nervousness was wreaking havoc on my system. Scott didn't mind. Lovingly, he placed a bracelet on my wrist. It was light and delicate with braided tan threads and smaller brown, cream, and light blue beads on top.

"Don't take it off until you come home to me in six months, Peggy, OK?" he asked. I knew I'd never take off that bracelet.

Scott and I went back to my parents' home, and I finished some last-minute packing. We spent the rest of the evening with my parents, talking around my childhood kitchen table. We were having such a wonderful time that it made me question my decision to leave for Colorado. *Why am I leaving this wonderful, handsome man?* He bonded with my parents, and it was making me miss them before I even left. We stayed up talking and laughing until midnight. When I went to bed, I wondered if it would be the last time sleeping in my childhood bedroom.

I filled my Volkswagen GTI to the roof, barely able to see out the windows. Then I hit the road early the next day with my mother. She came with me to keep me company and to stay in Vail for a couple of weeks, helping to take care of my brother David who was just recovering from knee surgery.

I hugged Scott and Dad in the garage, holding on to each of them for a long time. Reluctantly, I got in the driver's seat and my mother got in the passenger seat. As we pulled out of the garage, Scott and Dad both walked forward, following us to where the edge of the garage met the driveway. I could still see them standing there waving as I looked at my rear-view mirror and pulled on to the road.

Saying goodbye to Scott and Dad was difficult. They both looked sad. I felt terrible making my father cry and seeing Scott's sad face, which I had never seen on him before. But I knew in my heart that they understood, and that they were happy and excited for me. With that in mind, I slowly allowed my feelings of excitement to grow stronger than my feelings of sadness. By the time my mother and I crossed into Kansas, I only felt excitement. *One more state to go!*

My mother and I drove for three days, finally arriving in Vail. David worked at the luxurious alpine-style Sonnenalp Hotel, so we were able to stay for three weeks at a discounted rate. I loved being close to the village and walking the cobblestone roads to the shops and restaurants in Vail. I felt grateful we had a room facing the mountain, and I enjoyed opening the large windows, just staring out at the mountain. Keeping the windows open at night, I breathed in the crisp mountain air as I snuggled under my down comforter. I kept enough belongings to last me the next six months in a gorgeous armoire and thought how I'd love to have something like it in my future bedroom with Scott.

Landing a job wasn't a problem. I found plenty, but I couldn't find a place to live. So I settled on a position as a live-in nanny. The digs weren't too shabby. I had a bedroom, bathroom, and living room all to myself, as well as a gorgeous view of Beaver Creek, a world-class ski resort. Since my job didn't start for four weeks, I decided to surprise Scott and come home for a month.

I secretly told Scott's housemate about my plans and asked him to make sure Scott was home when I arrived. When I walked in the door, Scott was babysitting his housemate's children. He sat on the couch, a child under each arm, watching cartoons. Toys were strewn over the floor.

The children were in their pajamas and cuddled up to him like he was a big teddy bear. When he saw me, he looked as though he couldn't believe his eyes. At first, he couldn't speak. Finally, he told me, "I've never been so happy in my life."

I could tell Scott wanted to get off the couch quicker, but he had two children leaning on him and didn't want to hurt them by abruptly jumping up. Gently, he peeled them off of him. We ran toward each other, meeting halfway across the room in an embrace. He held me tightly, then stretched his arms out in front of him, a hand on each of my shoulders, looking at me as if to make sure it was really me before he celebrated further.

I spent the month at home solidifying our relationship. I even brought Scott to the Poconos, where we stayed in my family's camper. Then I introduced him to my childhood ski-and-bike buddies. I took him to restaurants and outdoor places that had become special to me over a lifetime of weekends. Somehow, though, being there with him made it feel like my first visit—the first time I shared it all with the man I loved.

We also spent time with our families and friends. We wanted to savor and maximize our time together. Yet Scott still had to work. So I drove him to work and picked him up at the end of the day. When he wasn't working, we explored hiking trails at Jockey Hollow at Morristown National Historical Park, Tripod Rock in the Pyramid Mountain Natural Historical Area, and Hacklebarney State Park. I felt thrilled to be with someone who appreciated the outdoors as much as I did.

I also enjoyed watching him play hockey late at night in his men's league. I was amazed at how quickly he could go from standing still on his skates to skating at full speed—how he could stop on a dime and turn very quickly. Given what he'd been through, his athleticism was all the more incredible. Watching him play with skill and confidence, and imagining touching those muscles that made him powerful, was a huge turn-on.

My parents got to know him better, too. Scott already was forging a friendship with my father. The two of them loved to watch Sunday night football together. During Giants games, Scott's hooting and howling rivaled that of my father. I felt good to see them enjoying each other's company without me even being in the room. I found it amusing and cute to think that my parents were inviting us over not only to see me, but so that my father could spend time with Scott. I felt touched by their developing closeness and friendship. We celebrated my father's birthday dinner at my parents' house, and Scott had everyone laughing with tears. They were both goofy, which is no doubt why they got along well. Scott loved to tell stories. He proudly told my father how he'd been given a pair of Rollerblades® that were too small. Rather than throw them away or give them to someone else with smaller feet, he cut the toe pieces off so his feet would fit.

Every night, I fell asleep with my head on Scott's shoulder and his arms wrapped around me. If we separated during the night, he pulled me close to him. I felt safe, protected, and loved.

Then reality struck: time for me to leave. Again. I didn't know how I was going to bear it, so we hatched a plan: Scott would visit me. My employers liked me and said it was fine for Scott to spend a week with me at their house.

About a month after I had settled in to my temporary home in Colorado, Scott came out to visit for a week just before Christmas. What a week!

One evening we took a moonlit open sleigh ride under blankets to a cabin on the mountain for a gourmet dinner. We went skiing, shopping, eating out, and, when I was on duty, took care of the adorable three-year-old girl for whom I was a nanny. "This is good practice for when we have our own children," Scott said. While I made the little girl lunch, he sat next to her on the couch and read to her. He showed her how he could wiggle his ears, and she laughed in delight.

The girl had a problem with her esophagus, so I had to cut up her food into tiny pieces. She could chew well, but sometimes her muscles did not move the food down properly, causing her to regurgitate. The problem was no cause for alarm. I learned that I could easily clean things up if I simply put my cupped hands in front of her to catch the small amount of regurgitated food, throw it in the garbage, and wash my hands. I let Scott know about her condition ahead of time, so he wouldn't be alarmed if it happened in front of him. It did happen, but before I could get to her with my hands, Scott was there. Without hesitation, he caught her regurgitated food in his cupped hands and didn't flinch. To me, this was one more demonstration of how he was going to make a wonderful, loving father—the kind of man I always dreamed of as the father of my children. I found myself loving him even more.

After Scott left, I was heartbroken. Although I was in the mountains skiing at two of the best ski resorts in the world, with a bedroom that overlooked the Rockies, I felt empty. I missed him terribly. My birthday was coming up, and Scott's was only two days later, so I thought it would be a great idea to ask my employer for that week off. Plus, the annual party at my home mountain in the Poconos was taking place that weekend. I thought I could see Scott for just one more week, come back, finish my time in Colorado, and I would be good. I didn't think one week off from work in a six-month period was too much to ask.

I approached her one evening after we were lingering around the dinner table. "Susan, my birthday is coming up, and my boyfriend's birthday is two days after mine. It also happens to be the same weekend as our annual picnic at our ski area. I would love to have the week off."

I was not prepared for her response. "Peggy," she said abruptly, "you cannot have the week off. When you took this job, you knew it was from November through April, with no time off. So no, you cannot have the week off." *OK, this is disappointing, but I can accept her decision.* To my surprise, she kept on talking. "I cannot believe that you cannot go six months without your boyfriend. You are mentally unstable!"

I was shocked at what she said and extremely disappointed that she didn't grant my request. But what really hurt me was being called "mentally unstable." I decided right then and there to quit—not so much because she denied me the week off, but because of what she'd called me. Mentally unstable. I simply could not work for her or live there any longer.

"Susan, I've been here for three months, loving your daughter and taking care of her as if she were my own. I have provided her with excellent care. Being newly in love and wanting to be with my boyfriend and requesting one week off in six months is not mentally unstable. I cannot work for someone who does not respect me and who insults me. I quit." Then she appeared to be the one in shock. I stunned myself, too. I had never quit anything in my life.

Without further discussion, I walked downstairs to my bedroom and immediately called my parents. "Mom," I cried, "I just quit my job. I'm coming home."

"What do you mean, dear? What happened?"

"The lady I work for called me mentally unstable. I cannot work, much less live in the same house, as someone who calls me mentally unstable."

"When will you come home?" my mother asked.

"Well, I don't want to leave them high and dry without someone to take care of their daughter, so I think I'll stay on for another week to give her time to find a replacement."

"I have an idea," my mother replied. "Dad and I just booked our vacation to visit you and David in four weeks. Maybe you can stay with David for a few weeks, then spend a week with us at the hotel, and then Dad or I can drive back home to New Jersey with you?"

I cried with relief as I listened to my mother's plan. "You're so smart, Mom! That sounds like a great idea." I went to bed emotionally exhausted, but also completely relieved that I had a plan. I also felt good about providing my employer with some time to find a replacement.

I didn't see Susan again until she came home from work the next day. I'm not sure why, but I have never had difficulty sticking up for myself. "Susan, I understand your point of view, but I simply cannot work for someone who insults me and does not respect me. I don't want to leave you without care for your daughter, so I can stay for a week to give you time to find someone."

Susan appeared much more calm and remorseful, but she did not apologize. "Well, that's great," she said, "because I already found someone who can start on Monday." No apology. No thank you. I knew I made the right decision.

I skied for twenty days straight and slept on my brother's couch with all my belongings in garbage bags shoved in a small hallway. When my parents finally arrived in Vail, I was thrilled to see them. I then spent a wonderful week skiing with my family. When it was over, we decided that my father would drive with me across the country this time.

When my mother and I made the trip, we did it in three days. My father and I left on February 13th, one day before Valentine's Day. I thought it would be really sweet to be with Scott on Valentine's Day. I quickly calculated how many hours we would have to drive each day in order to squeeze the trip into two days and arrive at my house by midnight on Valentine's Day. We wouldn't get much sleep, but we could do it!

We were driving through Salinas, Kansas, and making good time. I was so excited to see Scott, I could hardly wait! As my father was driving along the long stretch of straight and flat roadway, all of a sudden, we heard a deafening thumping noise. "What the heck was that?" I yelled. My father quickly pulled over and realized that we had blown a tire. I burst into tears on the side of the road, realizing we were now not going to make it home by Valentine's Day. My father excitedly pointed out, "Look! A twenty-four-hour truck stop right there! They must have tires!" We then got back in the car and slowly drove on the shoulder about an eighth of a mile to the exit. The truck stop was located immediately off of the exit. It couldn't have happened at a more convenient place!

At the truck stop, I had never seen so many tires in my life and smelled such a strong odor of rubber. It was so overwhelming that I began to get a headache. I wanted to hug the man behind the counter when he said that we would be on our way in less than two hours. While wonderful, that meant we would not arrive on Valentine's Day. "Dad, we're not going to make it," I said, accepting defeat. Although we knew that we were not going to make it by Valentine's Day, I still wanted to get home as soon as possible. I was so close to experiencing Scott's hug that I didn't want to wait one more minute than I had to.

We arrived home at 2:00 a.m. February 15. When I opened the door from my garage to my kitchen, I could see Scott through the kitchen into the family room, asleep on the couch. He was adorable, sleeping with his arms folded across his chest. As my father quietly went upstairs to greet my mother, I gently woke Scott up. "I'm very sorry I missed Valentine's Day," I whispered in his ear as I lay next to him.

"That's OK," he said, "You're home. Now we can begin our lives together." I was so tired that I didn't even bother changing. I kept on the clothes I was wearing and snuggled in beside him on the couch with my head on his shoulder and his strong arm wrapped around me. With the most comforting sense of peace, I quickly fell asleep.

Now that I was home to stay, I felt security in forever. As I busily looked for a job and studied for the Graduate Record Examinations, Scott focused on studying for his insurance license. No matter how hard he tried, though, he could not pass that damn test. I felt bad for him. He could beat anyone in solving the Rubik's Cube and answer every question correctly on *Jeopardy*, but he could not pass the test. Something about being in that car accident had affected his brain. He struggled silently, never letting on to anyone about his cognitive difficulties.

I noticed the problem because I spent so much time with him. He was concrete and literal in his thinking, highly organized, and had some short-term memory problems, which became clear one day when I arrived home from work. He did not have to work that day. I had mentioned to him things we needed to get done around the apartment, along with just a few items we needed from the grocery store. When I returned home from work, he had not done any of it. He seemed embarrassed and said he would do it tomorrow. I knew he had not sat around doing nothing because the apartment was spotless, just as he liked it.

The next day when I went to work, I reminded him of what needed to get done and what we needed from the grocery store. He suggested that I write it down. There were only two things that needed to be done in the apartment, but I wrote them down for him. There were only three things we needed from the store, but I made up a list. When I returned from work, he proudly showed me how he had fixed the drip in the kitchen sink and attached the phone to the wall. Then he opened the refrigerator and showed me how he purchased the milk, orange juice, and butter that we needed.

I learned to make lists for him and found his quirks endearing. I went to the local craft store and purchased a plain wooden plaque, a notepad, small wooden letters to spell our names, acrylic paint, small wire flowers, and a glue gun. I then made a decorative wall plaque to hang by the phone in our entryway. I glued one notepad to the plaque in the middle. Under it were our names, "Peggy" on the left and "Scott" on the right, to celebrate that this was our home. Now we would always have a notepad handy for our lists.

We settled into a nice life together. We both worked full time. I traveled to Newark to work with young children at a hospital-based preschool for children with significant behavioral and emotional problems at Newark Beth Israel Medical Center. Scott took the train to New York City to work in the customer service department for Dean Witter. We enjoyed an evening routine of dinner, a walk in the neighborhood, and the 11:00

news before falling asleep. On Tuesdays, we treated ourselves to all-you-can eat spaghetti at The Chatham Sandwich Shop. In our free time on weekends, we went hiking and biking, attended concerts, and spent time with family and friends. A simple life together. A beautiful life together.

In March of 1993, we were snowed in for the weekend at my parents' house. The roads were not safe for travel. My father was digging around in the basement for something. We all heard the rumblings and bangs and could not imagine what he was doing until he appeared at the top of the basement steps holding an old sled—the kind with a wooden top to sit on, an upside-down "V" to steer, and steel runners along the bottom.

"Let's go sledding!" he said. So Scott, my dad, and I dressed in our snow gear, with Scott borrowing many items from my father. Our driveway was not yet shoveled, so we trudged through eighteen inches of fresh snow down to Stone Fence Road, which had been plowed but was left with a solid two inches of packed snow and ice—perfect for riding a Flexible Flyer®. We thought we'd take turns before Scott and Dad decided to ride together.

I stood at the top of the hill, a spot I'd stood a hundred times with my bike as a child, the hill where we used to see how much speed we could get, the hill where my best friend, Jeriann, and I wore out our sneakers by dragging them so that our mothers would take us to the store to get matching sneakers. It was the very spot I wiped out on gravel, causing that fat lip that lasted for years.

Scott and Dad looked like a funny sight getting on that sled. My father lay down on his stomach, head first. Scott piled on top of him, and off they went—a pair of two hundred-pound men picking up speed as they flew down Stone Fence Road. Instead of their weight causing them to sink and slow, they accelerated faster and faster until they crashed, thankfully in a soft snowbank. No one was hurt, and they were smart enough not to test their luck and try another time.

In spring of 1993, Scott and I went whitewater rafting on the Lehigh River in Pennsylvania with my parents, my sister, my sister's boyfriend, and my brother. The dam had just been released, so the water was flowing quite swiftly. We changed into our wet suits, which were still damp and freezing cold from the last river trip. We all came out of the changing rooms in our wetsuits. I joked, "We look like the Sleestak, those lizard-like creepy creatures from that old TV show, 'Land of the Lost'!" Before departing for the trip, we listened to a brief tutorial about paddling and river safety.

I realized early on that this was not going to be a relaxing trip. My father was seated at the end of the raft. They warned us during the safety talk that this was the most likely position to get bounced out of the boat. Sure enough, after about ten minutes of being on the raft, my father got tossed into the river. As we unknowingly hit rocks, this happened a few more times. Each time it happened, Scott quickly went into action and was able to pull him back in. At one point both my father and Scott fell in the river at the same time. Scott wasn't available to pull my father out but, even worse, Scott didn't know how to swim. I was seated in the raft closest to where my father was in the river. I have no idea where I gained the strength, but somehow, I managed to pull my father back in. Once he was in, he quickly pulled Scott back in. We were all relieved but had no time to celebrate. We needed to pay attention and try not to hit any more rocks!

When some people thought Scott and I were engaged, he did not correct them. He'd even made a guest list for our wedding. When we walked his dog, he pointed out a house that he imagined us living in one day. He had nicknames for me. "Pegaroo," he'd say. Or "Peggyo!" On June 2, 1993, I wrote in my diary: "He has become a part of me. I can't imagine my life without him. In fact, the thought is frightening."

Scott was wonderful to live with. He even made grocery shopping romantic. Every morning he woke me up with his sweet kisses. As I headed off to work, Scott watched me go to my car in the parking lot behind our apartment. He'd stand in front of the floor-to-ceiling window in his white terry cloth robe. He looked so damn handsome in that robe, making it really hard to leave for work! He would call my name, get my attention, and then drop his robe, displaying his full nakedness. *Holy crap! I sure hope no one else sees this!* Then he'd turn around and wiggle his butt at me, looking over his shoulder and smiling. I loved his goofiness. I loved how he wanted to make me smile as I went off to work. I loved his body! It didn't matter how many times he did this. Each time, he got the same reaction out of me—our special little ritual that made me grin, every single time.

My sister got married in November 1993. At her storybook wedding (the kind I dreamed of), I caught the bouquet! Then Scott asked me to marry him seven weeks later! When my father heard that Scott had proposed, he immediately told me the story of how Scott had asked him for his blessing. Apparently, at the end of my sister's wedding reception, Scott helped load the wedding gifts into my father's Bronco. He seemed nervous until he finally spoke.

"You know me by now, Dr. Doherty," he said. "You know I'm a good man. I love your daughter and would like to marry her." My father was touched that Scott felt comfortable talking to him about his plans to propose to me.

"What do you mean?" my father joked. "My wallet is still burning from this wedding!" They shook hands and hugged.

Seven weeks later, on December 24, 1993, Scott proposed to me. It was the happiest day of my life. Scott had to work that day. As he left at 7:00 a.m., he turned on my nightstand lamp. The light shone brightly in my eyes. I couldn't open them to look at him. "Why are you turning the light on?" I asked, slightly annoyed. I had the day off, and I was finally able to sleep in!

At my bedside, he then got down on one knee. "This is why," he said. "I turned the light on so that you could see your ring. Will you marry me? Will you do me the honor of being my wife?"

Since I'd just been abruptly woken up and was still adjusting to the light, I felt slightly confused about what he'd said. After a moment, it hit me. *He's asking me to marry him!* "Yes! Yes! I will marry you!" I pulled my covers off and leaned over to give him a hug, just as he was standing up to give me a hug. We embraced tightly, and I cried on his shoulder.

We had talked about getting married, but this totally took me by surprise! "I wanted to do something special to propose," Scott said. "But I just couldn't wait anymore to ask and give this ring to you. And I know we're seeing your parents and friends tonight for Christmas Eve. I wanted us to be able to tell everyone tonight!" He then gently put the ring on my finger and proudly explained that the diamond was from his father's mother's engagement ring. "I designed the rest myself," he added. "These are sapphire baguettes." *He's so cute talking about baguettes.* It was very characteristic for Scott to propose in such a simple manner. His simplicity was part of what I loved about him. And it was also characteristic of him to be somewhat impulsive. He simply could not wait to give it to me. I found that endearing, and his eagerness to propose meant more to me than a fancy proposal.

We decided to get married on March 18, 1995 at the same place my sister had her reception, Stronghold Mansion in Bernardsville. Those were the days I'd dreamed of since I was a little girl—long hours perusing bridal magazines, shopping for a wedding dress, and planning our honeymoon along the Pacific Coast Highway in California, where we'd spend our first days as husband and wife.

# The Last Summer

## February 1994

Three months after he proposed to me, Scott found the lump. That night, I could not wait to get to my parents' house for our usual Sunday night family meal. I needed that familiar comfort. I needed to be told the lump was nothing to worry about.

When my dad looked at it, though, his face lost its color and his almost permanent smile faded. He was a psychiatrist, but he still knew a thing or two about anatomy and pathology.

"What do you think, Dad?" I asked. "The lump appeared overnight!" He looked away from me for a second or two and swallowed.

"I'm not sure," he said, "but, Scott, you really need to get that checked out. Tomorrow."

"I'm sure it's nothing," Scott replied, "but just to appease you all, I'll go. But you know I hate doctors." I tried to make a joke to lighten the awfulness of the situation.

"What? You hate doctors? My dad is one, and I'm going to be one." Scott didn't smile. Neither did my dad. I felt again the tears I held back when Scott had first showed me the lump on his neck. I wanted to break down and cry. *Please God, don't let anything be wrong with him. He is my fiancé. I love him. We're getting married.* Scott agreed to call in the morning and make an appointment. His willingness to see a doctor scared me. *What is he feeling? What is he not telling me?* My dad always hugged me before I left the house, but that night his arms held me tighter, his embrace lasted longer than usual.

The next day Scott went to his family doctor, who tested him for mononucleosis and strep throat. As we waited for the results, Scott felt worse and worse. He had neither condition. Because he felt awful, he went back to the doctor four days later. His neck was so swollen that he was having trouble breathing.

Finally, as his health continued to decline, Scott was admitted to a hospital. His family doctor didn't know what was wrong with him. When I visited, his spirits were high. Scott simply didn't know any other way to be. I was a wreck, though. I left that day, still not knowing what was wrong. Later, Scott's mother called to tell me the doctors thought he had Hodgkin's disease, but they still didn't know for sure. I cried hard all night, resulting in the biggest headache of my life.

I had to pull myself together, though, because I had an interview at a university the next day. I'd been preparing for that day for years. I was granted six interviews for six different psychology doctoral programs. Five of the six were scheduled for that very week. Scott encouraged me to go, knowing how hard I'd worked to get into a doctoral program.

Nevertheless, my interviews went poorly. I couldn't concentrate or stop thinking about Scott. It was so difficult to fight back tears. While at Rutgers University, I had to write an essay. I have never experienced such difficulty concentrating in my life. I knew that my essay did not make any sense whatsoever. But I felt like I had to write something.

I then had a group interview. We had to talk a little bit about ourselves, and I simply could not keep it together anymore. The facilitator of the interview said, "Let's go around the room, with each of you saying a little bit about yourselves. What's your background? What interests you in this program? Where are you in your life right now?"

Before it was even my turn in the group interview, I broke down. *Where am I at in my life right now? I'm in hell. My fiancé has cancer, and I'm terrified that he's going to die.* The professors and other candidates demonstrated genuine concern and compassion, which only made me cry more. "Excuse me," I said, exiting the group interview briefly to gain my composure. I was able to return to the interview, but I was pretty sure I just blew my chances of getting in. And it scared me that I didn't care.

I also had an individual interview at Seton Hall University with two professors. Once again, I could not concentrate. My eyes were so puffy from crying the night before that I felt like they were half-shut. I knew I wasn't making sense with my interview responses, and I struggled with whether to tell the professors what I was going through. In the moment, I chose not to. Afterwards, I called one of the professors to let her know that I'd just found out the night before that my fiancé might have cancer, explaining why I was not able to articulate myself clearly and requesting another interview. My request was denied. I did not get into the program. I'd had only one interview scheduled before Scott found the lump. I'd rocked that one at Pace University, and that was the only program that accepted me.

Scott needed a biopsy of his lump to make a formal diagnosis. That whole week, we wavered between accepting he had cancer and hoping for something else. While waiting, smaller lumps appeared all over his head. I could tell he was scared.

Scott remained in the hospital all week. I wanted to spend the day with him, but I had to return to the preschool program where I worked. I'd missed so many days to do my interviews. I needed to get back to work. When I couldn't be with Scott, my sweet mother went instead. I called Scott during my break between the morning class and the afternoon class when the children were not there, to see if there was any news about the biopsy. There was. Scott gave me the news in a very matter-of-fact manner.

"Peggy," he said.

"Yes?" I replied, dreading what he was about to say next.

"I have cancer." I screamed, causing my coworkers to rush into the classroom to see what was wrong. I know my outburst was not what he needed, but I could not stop crying.

"Don't worry," he said in true Scott form. "Everything is going to be OK." But I didn't believe him. My concerned coworkers all stood around me, touching me and comforting me. They didn't know yet what was wrong, but they knew it must be bad. Then my mom got on the phone.

"Peggy, everything is going to be all right," she said. "Scott is handling the news well. He is more concerned about you. He is going to be fine." I wanted to believe her, but I didn't. I wanted to rush right to the hospital to be with Scott.

"There's no need for you to come here," he said. "They're sending me home. I should be there in a few hours. Meet me at home." I was confused. *If he has cancer, why is he coming home?* It was as if he read my mind.

"They want me to get the best treatment for the kind of cancer I have, and that is at Westchester County Medical Center," he explained. *I can't believe we're talking about this. What kind of cancer? Where the hell is Westchester County Medical Center?* I didn't want to upset Scott with any questions, so I just said I'd be waiting for him at home.

"I love you, and I'll be waiting for you at home," I said, over and over again.

I hung up the phone and was comforted by the hugs of ten or so loving women. I couldn't speak, but I didn't need to. They heard enough to understand that Scott was very sick and that I needed to go home and be with him.

❄ ❄ ❄

Waiting there for him to come home seemed like the longest two hours of my life. Scott walked through the door, just as he'd done so many times. He did not look sick. *Maybe they've got it all wrong*, I thought. *Maybe he really doesn't have cancer.* Scott was very matter-of-fact.

"The doctors said, 'Just enjoy yourself. Do whatever you want. We'll see you on Monday.'"

"Where Monday? Where is this place?" I asked.

"Some hospital in New York. I really don't know, but the best doctors to treat what I have are there." I noticed that he didn't say "cancer." *He's thinking what I'm thinking: maybe if we don't say it, it won't be true.* "So what do you want to do?" I just wanted to hug him and make the cancer go away. I was not sure how he felt or what he was up to doing.

"Whatever you want to do," I said. "What do you want to do?" He became animated.

"Let's get Chinese food!" That's something we'd done several times before on a Friday night, and I believe that it was his way of acting as though everything was normal. But things were so not normal. I didn't want him to drive to pick up the food, but I also didn't want to leave him alone in the apartment.

"I'll drive, but I want you to come with me," he said, as if sensing my insecurity. We drove in silence, which felt uncomfortable because it was so unusual for us. I was afraid that if I opened my mouth, I'd choke on my words, and only sobs would come out. We rode without speaking to and from the Chinese restaurant, went home, and ate.

"Let's open our fortune cookies," I said. "I'll go first." I unwrapped the cookie and read aloud: "'Challenging and adventurous things are coming your way.'" *I don't know about adventurous, but challenging, for sure.* Scott looked at me and winked. He reached for his cookie, crumpled it open, and read.

"'You are headed in the right direction,'" he read. *Thank God.*

As soon as we finished eating our Chinese food, Scott said he wanted friends to come over. He wanted it to be like any other Friday night. By 8:00, Debbie and Don, Charlie and Linda, Laura Leigh, John Ryan, Chris, Jennifer and Greg, and Nancy all arrived, and they all stayed until midnight. To my surprise, Scott wanted to invite friends over Saturday night as well. So once again, we had a little party, with Doug, Chris, Charlie and Linda, Nancy, and Jennifer. As always, he was upbeat and spirited and assured everyone he would be fine. No one could tell anything was wrong with him except for his big swollen neck. It was the elephant in the room that no one mentioned.

Sleeping was difficult for Scott. He was unable to get comfortable. We tried propping him up with pillows so he could keep his chest up. That didn't help. He coughed so hard that it scared me. It sounded like he could barely breathe or swallow. I didn't sleep at all. I stayed awake that whole first night in case he stopped breathing. I think neither of us got an hour of sleep. When he woke up, he wanted to make love. I didn't think it was a good idea. He was coughing hard and having difficulty breathing while just lying there. I couldn't imagine how he could possibly muster the energy to make love. I was certain that he would have even more difficulty breathing and not be able to stop coughing. That was the first time I ever turned him down. It made me very sad.

That Sunday before Scott entered the hospital to begin treatment, we spent time with his two best friends, his family, and my family. Throughout the day, Scott looked very uncomfortable. It hurt to see him suffering. He coughed a lot. We prolonged our usual Sunday night dinner at my parents' house. They tried hard to make the meal a typical Doherty Sunday dinner, but there was nothing normal about it. "I made you the pea soup you love," my mother said. My mother learned early on in my relationship with Scott that if there was going to be any food for the rest of us, she first had to fill Scott and my dad up with hearty soup. But tonight Scott barely touched it. He hardly ate anything at all. I tried hard to ignore his swollen neck.

We pretended, all of us. "How are the Rangers doing this season?" my father asked Scott. My father had no interest in hockey. I knew he was trying to lighten the conversation and elevate Scott's spirits by asking him about one of his passions, The New York Rangers hockey team. I felt my parents' worry. I could see that my mother was biting her lower lip, trying to hold back her tears. My own worry made me sick to my stomach. I couldn't eat a thing. I felt like a little kid, playing around with my food and covering it with a napkin, so Scott wouldn't see that I couldn't eat.

"Excuse me," Scott said, abruptly getting up from the table and going right to the bathroom, which shared a wall with the kitchen. Just on the other side of that wall, we could hear Scott vomiting. I couldn't hold it together anymore. I just looked at my parents and cried. Scott came out of the bathroom. "Don't worry, Carol," he joked. "It wasn't your cooking." Then he winked at my mother.

Since no one was eating, and the conversation felt difficult, we decided to clean up the table and go into the family room to watch a movie. This alone felt strange. Our usual scenario was to linger, tell jokes and funny stories, and laugh until our stomach muscles hurt. Scott and I sat next to each other all night and held hands really tightly. It was as if we didn't want to let go of each other. Ever.

I got out of bed Monday with fear and dread. Neither of us had gotten any sleep, as Scott got up several times in the night throwing up. My heart ached for him. My heart ached for me. I could hear him in the bathroom when I woke up. Slowly approaching the bathroom, I asked cautiously, "How are you feeling, dear?"

To my surprise, he had just taken a shower. He looked so handsome in his terrycloth robe, loosely belted, exposing his muscular chest. There he stood, right in the same spot where he first showed me the lump just two weeks ago. Only now, a large bandage covered the incision from the biopsy, and his entire neck was swollen. "I feel great! Want to make love?" *Oh my God; I love this man so much. He is so brave.*

I wasn't sure if we should. I didn't know if it would hurt him, but I was even more scared not to. I had no idea what we were in for once we got to the hospital and his treatment began. Then my cruel mind thought that this might be our last time to make love because he might die. "Are you sure you're feeling up for it? You know I find you irresistible, but I'm worried about you." I tried hard to hold back my tears. My lips quivered, my face contorted, and I could feel my eyes welling up with tears. Then a single tear released and streamed down my face, landing on the floor.

"Please don't cry," he pleaded. "I feel great, and I want to make love to my fiancé." He teased, "I'm pretty sure they won't allow us to do this in the hospital bed!" *Always a joker.*

He came closer to me, taking both of my hands into his, and he squeezed my hands while looking into my eyes. In silence, he dropped one hand to wipe away my tears, gently guiding me toward our bedroom with the other hand. We got to the edge of the bed, he untied his robe, and dropped it to the floor. I remembered all the times he had done that while standing in the window, shaking his butt at me and waving as I sat in the parking lot leaving for work. I felt overcome with emotion, thinking about how our lives were about to change as we ventured into the awful unknown of cancer treatment.

Scott lay down on the bed, softly pulling me next to him. We made love, and it was just as passionate, tender, and loving as always, if not more so. This lovemaking session was overwhelmingly meaningful to me, as I could not get rid of that cruel thought that it might be the last time because he might die before leaving the hospital. He made love to me with such passion and intention that I wondered if he had also imagined it might be our final time together.

All the way to the hospital in the back seat of his parents' Saab, we held hands. I didn't want to let go of him. Oh, how I wished we were being taken on some romantic date and not to the hospital to start chemotherapy treatment. The leather seats in the car were cold; I already felt chilled and couldn't bear the thought of being without him. I didn't know how long I'd be allowed to stay with him at the hospital, so I brought a small bag with a toothbrush and change of clothes, just in case I was allowed to stay overnight. My small bag sat on the seat next to me, with Scott sitting close to me on the other side.

The ninety-minute ride seemed to take forever. We didn't talk much at all. His parents didn't, either. The dread in all of us was palpable. I felt bad for Scott. I felt bad for his parents, taking their only son to begin treatment for cancer. I felt bad for myself. The love of my life was sick. Very sick.

We drove over the Tappan Zee Bridge, crossing the Hudson River below, leaving New Jersey and entering New York. The day was clear. On such days, I always looked to the right when I got close to the toll booths to see the New York City skyline. That day, I didn't care to see it. I just prayed that the hospital was not too much farther away. I already felt so far away from home.

After driving another fifteen minutes, we turned off the highway into a residential neighborhood and then into a large hospital parking lot. We parked in front of the hospital in a lot with a sign that read: "Visitors." *Yes, visitors. Just visitors. That's what we all are. In and out, and Scott will be home in no time at all.*

We walked inside the sterile, cold hospital and waited for just a few minutes for the doctor to call us in. Scott's oncologist said he had a very aggressive type of cancer. If left untreated, it would kill him in two weeks. Scott would receive chemotherapy in the hospital for the next three to four weeks.

There was more: Scott would need a bone marrow transplant in three months. His sisters each had a 25 percent chance of being a match. If they weren't, Scott would go on a list to find a match, which could take six months—time he didn't have.

The oncologist then said the most awful words I've ever heard: Scott had a 15 percent chance of survival. I felt like I was going to die right there. If Scott wasn't in the room, I would have fallen to the floor, but I could not let Scott see me so devastated. Then and there, the journey started. He needed me to be strong, beginning that very moment.

A nurse escorted Scott right from the oncologist's office to begin his treatment. We hugged before he left. "I'll see you in a few hours, sweetie," I said, trying desperately to be brave for him. He winked at me, and he was gone.

"He'll be in Room 714," the nurse said as she guided Scott out of the room. "You can meet him there in a few hours. The cafeteria is just down the hall. The food is pretty decent." Scott's parents and I gathered up our belongings and headed toward the cafeteria. I had absolutely no appetite, but I was able to swallow a few sips of hazelnut coffee.

We waited three hours in the cafeteria, which felt like an eternity. "How about if we go up now?" Mrs. Unger suggested. "If he's not there yet, I'm sure we can wait for him there." We left the cafeteria, walking down the long sterile hallway to the elevator. I stood closest to the buttons and reluctantly pushed number seven for the oncology floor. *I don't want to go there. I don't want to go there.*

We stepped out of the elevator and were greeted by a sign, "Oncology." I didn't want to go any farther. *We don't belong here. Scott doesn't belong here.* We slowly walked to Room 714. Mrs. Unger opened the door. She looked back at me over her shoulder. I felt her concern. Instead of walking directly into his room as I expected, we walked into a tiny vestibule with a sink and another door leading to Scott's room. I could see Scott on the bed through the small window of the door. A sign instructed us to wash our hands and put on the yellow flimsy hospital gown. I didn't understand why.

Mrs. Unger led the way, followed by Mr. Unger, and then me. Scott was propped up in his hospital bed, watching The Sports Network. He smiled, appearing to be in good spirits. "You found me! I was wondering when you were going to get here!" he said. The curtain was drawn, and I could hear that he had a roommate on the other side of the curtain. I imagined an old, sickly man on the other side. I approached Scott quietly and gave him a kiss on the cheek.

"How are you feeling?" I asked quietly. I didn't want to disturb the old, sick man on the other side. To my surprise, I heard the sound of the curtain being opened quickly, as it moved along the metal track on the ceiling and made a whooshing sound. Then I was even more surprised at what I saw.

"Hello there!" the young man said with excitement. "I'm Kevin. And this is my fiancé, Susan." Kevin was bald and handsome, and sitting up in bed. Susan sat facing him on the edge of his bed, leaning toward him. I noticed her beautiful, thick blonde hair.

"I was wondering when I was going to get a roommate!" Kevin exclaimed. *Holy crap! He looks younger than Scott. Why the hell is he here?* "Sorry you all have to wear that yellow gown. That's because of me." Kevin was very friendly and had a lot of energy. "I just had a bone marrow transplant," he said. "I've got Hodgkin's Lymphoma. No, I *had* Hodgkin's Lymphoma. But my immune system is compromised. So to minimize my chance of infection, they make you wear the gowns." He paused, as if giving us a moment to take everything in, adding, "Oh, it's fine. Just don't use the bathroom!"

I just wanted to focus on Scott, but now I found myself also concerned about this young, bald, handsome man. *How long had he been there? How serious was his condition? How was this beautiful couple managing with cancer treatment during their engagement like we were?* I felt terribly saddened that this engaged couple was facing the same dire circumstances that we were. And I was selfishly comforted that Scott had a young, vibrant, friendly roommate and not the old, sickly one that I had imagined.

"I'm hungry!" Scott said. "I need to eat now. I can't wait until my dinner comes, and it's probably crappy anyway. Mom, would you mind getting me something to eat?" Scott's mother and father then left the room, giving two engaged couples time to connect and get to know each other.

I walked over to Susan. Instead of shaking her hand, I gave her a hug. I felt an instant connection with her. I sensed that she was grateful to meet us. After all, it's not every day that you meet someone in her twenties who is also engaged to a man in treatment for cancer. Whether we liked it or not, we shared a bond. I walked over to Kevin. I wasn't sure how close I should get, or whether I could touch him. As if he sensed my uncertainty, he extended his arm to shake my hand. Since Scott was stuck in his bed, attached to the pole administering his chemotherapy, he just watched and smiled.

"How far along are you in your bone marrow transplant?" I asked Kevin. Scott is going to need one in a few months. "I should be out of here in two weeks," Kevin said proudly. "And then I should be totally fine. Hodgkin's Lymphoma has about a 90 percent survival rate. What kind of cancer do you have, Scott?" he asked boldly.

"I've got Non-Hodgkin's Lymphoma. I suppose I'll be looking like you soon!" he joked, referring to Kevin's bald head.

"Yes, and I have some suggestions for you," Kevin said. "It felt really good for me to take control. So before my hair came out, I shaved it myself. That was really fun. I felt like a badass." He continued, "And here are a bunch of books you should read," pointing to his stack of self-help books. With a quick glance, I saw *Full Catastrophe Living*; *You Don't Have the Luxury of a Negative Thought*; *Love, Medicine, and Miracles*; and *Peace, Love, and Healing*.

"I'm not much of a reader," Scott said, "but maybe Peggy would like to read them." Scott glanced at me and moved his eyebrows up and down quickly. He knew that I knew that he had absolutely no interest in reading!

"And here's something they don't tell you," Kevin added. "If you want to have children, the first thing you should do when you get out of here is go to the sperm bank. If you go then, you'll still have a decent chance of having some strong sperm left."

I was shocked at how intimate and personal the conversation had become. But I was even more dismayed that no one mentioned this to us. If we had known, we would have gone to the sperm bank BEFORE the chemotherapy started! I was so worried about Scott, that not being able to have children had not even crossed my mind. Children meant a lot to me. I had been working with children since I was fourteen years old. I was determined not to let Scott see that this conversation tore my heart out. I was afraid that my feelings would betray my intentions as I spoke, so I kept it short and sweet. "Thank you for the suggestion, Kevin," was all that I could say, as I squeezed Scott's hand with all my might.

Scott's parents entered the room with some delicious hot spaghetti and meatballs for their son. I felt happy he had his appetite, wondering how long it would last. "Thanks, Mom," he said. He was very hungry and began eating immediately, almost oblivious to the rest of us in the room. Unfortunately, feeling well with an appetite was short-lived. "Peggy, quick. Hand that to me," Scott said, pointing to the little mauve-colored, kidney-shaped, plastic throw-up bin. I quickly brought it to him. He brought it up to his mouth and threw up. My relief that he was feeling better was suddenly shattered. I found a napkin and tenderly wiped his mouth as he leaned back in his bed in defeat.

Kevin saw what was going on and said, "Don't worry, man. It may get worse, but then it gets better. Soon, you're going to feel much better, and you'll have to request two meals for dinner to match your appetite."

The words of this sweet man we just met comforted me and offered Scott some hope for the future.

A few minutes after Scott threw up, his doctor came in. "How are you feeling, Scott," he asked. "You're not lookin' too good."

"My eyes were bigger than my stomach," Scott said. "I was so hungry. I must have eaten too fast." A nurse then walked in and introduced herself. "Hey there, kiddo," she said with her Irish accent. "I'm Eileen. I'm going to be your nurse for the evening." Then she walked over to the white board and wrote her name in big letters.

"I think it's time you got some rest," Scott's doctor said solemnly. "You've had a long day, and you've got some long days ahead. We need you as strong as you can be. A family member is allowed to stay, but I suggest that for tonight, everyone go home and get some rest."

Before the doctor left, Scott said, "Peggy's allowed too? She's my fiancé. She's family." He started off with a question, as if needing reassurance from the doctor that I was considered family. I noticed that he ended with a statement. I was his family. I could feel my tears welling up in my eyes, but I was determined not to cry in front of Scott.

As difficult as it was to leave, we decided that the doctor was right. Scott needed to rest. Then I noticed that I was exhausted, and I needed sleep too. Saying good night to Scott was hard. He looked sick and sad. I hated leaving him alone. His eyes were closed. I leaned in closer to him, pressing as much of my body against him as I could without causing him any discomfort. I whispered in his ear, "I'm leaving now, but I'll be back first thing in the morning. You won't even know I'm gone. Now you get some rest. I love you, my dear." He didn't have the energy to respond verbally and simply squeezed my hand. I heard his "I love you, too" in that squeeze.

Pulling myself off of him was one of the hardest things I have ever had to do in my life. I had to do it quickly, and I couldn't look back. I could not bear to. As soon as I left his room and knew that he couldn't hear me, I cried. I sobbed. I cried all the way down the hallway to the elevator. I cried as we went down seven floors in the elevator. I cried in the back seat of his parents' car all the way home. I cried saying goodbye to his parents in their driveway before I got in to my car to drive a half hour to my parents' home. I cried coming home and hugging my parents, who had been waiting up for me. My parents could see how exhausted I was. My mom said, "We love you. We love Scott. We'll talk in the morning." I quickly changed into my pajamas. These were the pajamas that I had packed in my overnight bag with the hopes that I would somehow be able to sleep next to Scott. I cried in my bed in my childhood bedroom, all alone. I had never felt so lonely or afraid.

I woke up in the morning and barely had the energy to get out of bed. I felt weak standing up, but somehow, I managed to take a shower and get dressed. I came downstairs to the kitchen, where my parents were having breakfast. "Here, have a bagel," my mom said, "or some fruit."

"Thanks, Mom, but I just don't have an appetite. I can't eat. But I will have some hazelnut coffee." I sat down with my coffee and gave my parents a brief synopsis of the previous day. Crying, I said to my parents, "He looked awful when I left. How can this be happening?" I could not speak any more and, cupping my face in my hands, I leaned over the kitchen table, where we had shared thousands of meals with laughter. My parents lovingly stroked my back and shoulders. I sensed that they wanted to say that everything was going to be OK, but it was becoming increasingly difficult to believe this to be true.

I allowed myself to consider the seriousness of his condition as I informed my parents what the doctor said. I took a deep breath and told them. "The doctor said that he will need a bone marrow transplant." I could barely speak through my sobs. "He said . . . that Scott . . . only . . . has . . . a 15 percent chance . . . of . . . liv . . . ing."

My parents couldn't speak either. The three of us just held each other and cried. After I cried every tear in me, I raised my head and wiped away the last tear on my face. "I have to be strong for Scott," I told my parents with determination. "I have to have hope." Reluctantly, I realized hope was all I had. I had no other way to cope with the days ahead, telling myself that a horrific car accident and lightning strike hadn't defeated Scott. If anyone could beat cancer, he could.

When Scott was in the hospital, I visited him every day. My employer was kind enough to let me work part time so that I could make this happen.

One day we were able to spend a lot of time alone without many nurses and doctors coming and going. He slept. I read my book, sitting as close to him as I could. When he woke up, he looked over at me and smiled. As I wrote in my journal and jotted down the date: March 18. I realized that was the day of our wedding the following year. "What day is it?" I asked Scott. Although he was confused from the heavy drugs and high from the synthetic marijuana helping his nausea and pain, he knew. "One year," he said, smiling. "One year, Peg."

Scott allowed visitors whenever he was feeling up for them. At times he had trouble talking, so he expressed his love and silliness by winking and sticking out his tongue at me. I set up his bulletin board in front of him. I selected pictures from his photo albums that I thought he would like, along with the many cards people sent him. He had difficulty standing, so I was shocked the next day to see the bulletin board had been rearranged. He'd placed an 8" x 10" photograph of the two of us on the bulletin board, separate from all the other photos. Also, he'd taken out another picture of me and put it on the board. I have no idea where he got that picture. "I want to wake up and see your smiling face every day," he said.

On April 5, 1994, Scott was discharged, and we were able to experience some normalcy for a while. He enjoyed roller blading with his friends on a deserted tennis court in the woods, bike riding through the shaded Loantaka Park, and watching the Rangers play hockey. I had never been a hockey fan, but Scott transformed me into one that spring. We had parties at our apartment every time a game came on television. I couldn't wait to get home from work, buy snacks and beer for our friends, and watch the game. Scott was the biggest Rangers fan I knew. When they won the Stanley Cup, we were all excited!

He really wanted to attend the Rangers parade in New York City on June 17. I begged him not to go, as he had thrown up in the morning before I went to work. I didn't want to go to work after he threw up. "Go to work, dear. Don't worry. I won't go if I feel sick."

When I arrived home at 4:00 after work, he wasn't there. He left me a note on the "Scott and Peggy" notepad that I made for us. "I feel great. I'm going to the parade," it read. I was relieved that he felt well enough to go and happy for him that he was going to see the parade of a lifetime. I made dinner and waited patiently for him to come home. When Scott got home, he didn't look well. He had beads of sweat on his forehead and sweat marks on his shirt. "Are you OK," I asked with more fear in my voice than concern. "You're sweating so much!"

Scott quickly sat down on a chair in our tiny kitchen—an uncomfortable choice, but the nearest place to sit. He lifted up the bottom of his shirt to his forehead and wiped away the beads of sweat so that they would not roll into his eyes. Although he did not look well, he was excited to tell me about his day. "I climbed a lamp post!" he said. "Everyone thought I was drunk!" he laughed.

"Why did they think you were drunk?"

"Well, I puked on the street, just like other people were puking on the street! They were drunk, and they thought I was drunk too!"

"You threw up? You told me you weren't going to go if you didn't feel well! You threw up? And now you're sweating like crazy. Let me take your temperature." I placed the thermometer in his mouth and patiently waited. I was upset. He had a fever of 103.

"Scott! You have a fever of 103! You threw up! You should not have gone!" I was angry that he'd gone and afraid of what the fever and vomiting meant.

He looked sick and defeated. "I had to go. The Rangers won the Stanley Cup! They won the Stanley Cup!" As he sat shaking, my anger dissipated, and I only felt fear. I called the doctor, who told me to bring Scott to the emergency room. Before getting off the phone, it dawned on me that I should ask which emergency room—the one nearby or the one an hour and a half away where he had his first round of chemotherapy? The doctor gave me the answer I didn't want to hear: "Westchester." Off we went to the emergency room, an hour and a half away.

It took hours for Scott to be seen. I was very upset, sitting there with him and having nothing I could do to relieve his pain and nausea. We sat, helpless, watching the police chase O.J. Simpson on the waiting room television on what was to become a historical Friday night in June. An emergency room doctor finally saw Scott. He prescribed him an antibiotic for an unknown infection and sent him home.

The next night, we slept on the floor in his parents' family room, the only room in their house with an air conditioner. The heat in our apartment was unbearable and made Scott, who was already sick and uncomfortable, feel even worse. Thankfully, Scott fell asleep quickly once we settled in the family room, but I lay awake, crying and worrying, *What's going to happen to him? What's going to happen to me?* My parents were in Europe. I wished they weren't. I wanted my mommy and daddy.

They were still away on the Fourth of July, the day of Chatham's big annual parade—one of Scott's favorites, though he was too sick to attend. He ran a fever that morning, and we were out of Tylenol. So I got in my car and made a right turn from our apartment onto Main Street toward the pharmacy. I headed up the hill and was stopped at the light. The parade had already begun, blocking off the road to the pharmacy. I could see it, but I couldn't get to it. The police officer directed me to turn left onto Hillside Avenue. *Please, just let me through!* The sign for the drugstore was right in front of me: Liberty Drug. But I had to turn left, going farther from where I needed to be. Then the parking lots were blocked off. I thought about just parking in some stranger's driveway. Finally, I found a place to park. I wasn't sure if I was in a legal spot, but I didn't care. I ran toward the pharmacy as fast as I could, with my backpack swinging back and forth on my back.

The closer I got to Main Street, the louder the parade got, overwhelming my senses. People lined the sidewalks, both standing and in lawn chairs. I could barely get by. Everyone and everything seemed in my way—happy people, a fire truck with the siren blaring, flags waving, horns honking. *Don't they know he's sick?* I tripped on a dog leash, fell, and got up with tears streaming down my face. Concerned strangers helped me up, saw my tears, and thought I was injured. I wasn't physically hurt, but inside, I was experiencing the biggest sadness of my life. I couldn't say a word. I just kept going toward that pharmacy to get that Tylenol.

On one awful day that summer, Scott had to have his bone marrow extracted. He lost so much blood during the procedure that he needed another blood transfusion. So we weren't able to leave the hospital until very late. Once he was discharged, I carefully helped him hobble down the long hallway. He remained bent at the waist in pain. With one arm around me, he leaned on me and grimaced in pain with each small step. *I can't do this. This is too much for me. He is too heavy for me. This is too*

*much pain.* I worried that I wasn't strong enough and that we would both fall to the hard floor. I have no idea why he didn't have a wheelchair. He probably told them that he didn't need one.

Once we got outside, I didn't want him to have to walk the long distance to the car. Yet I didn't want to leave him there by himself while I went and got the car. *He can't even stand by himself. I can't leave him here. He can't walk to the car. I don't know what to do. Help. Somebody tell me what to do.* I turned around, and through the glass doors, I waved my free arm around like a crazy lady, trying to summon a nurse.

Thankfully, she came outside to our aid. "He just had bone marrow extracted from his back. He's in so much pain. Please just hold him up while I go and get the car." I quickly got the car, drove to him, stopped, turned the car off, and got out of the car to help him. I wasn't sure which would be more comfortable for him, the front seat reclining, or the backseat lying down. "Honey, where do you want to sit?" He was in so much pain, he couldn't even respond. He leaned toward the passenger front door, indicating that he wanted to sit in the front. As we guided him into the car, Scott screamed in pain. Inside me, it felt like the pain was splitting my own heart in half.

With every bump and turn during that ninety-minute car ride, Scott screamed out in agony. *How am I going to get him home? Why is this happening? I'm not strong enough to do this!*

We were instructed to change his dressings the next day, so I gave Scott a bath to help lessen the grip of the sticky bandages. Because there was no hot water in the apartment that day, I heated water in pots on the stove and made several trips back and forth to fill the bathtub. I helped lower Scott slowly into the tub. Immediately, the water turned bright red with his blood. After twenty minutes, I helped him stand to get out of the tub. His body quivered and trembled in pain as blood trickled down his legs, leaving streaks. In his eyes was a sadness and desperation I'd never seen. I held him up, pulled off the dressing, and helped him to the bedroom.

As he lay face down on the bed, I did my best to tenderly peel off the bandages that covered deep holes across his back—holes so deep I couldn't see where they ended. I was very scared at what I saw and what I had to do to take care of him. I wanted help. I wanted someone else there to do this, or someone else to tell me that I was doing the right things. But he only wanted me. When I suggested that I get some help, he said, "I don't want anyone else to see me like this. I only want you." Inside, I wept, crying for many reasons. I felt touched that he only wanted me. I also felt deeply saddened that he was in this much pain. I was terrified that I didn't know how to take care of him by myself.

Somehow, a few days later, Scott was able to attend a Grateful Dead concert. Another couple had given us tickets as an engagement present. Scott was not going to pass on the opportunity to see his favorite band. Once the concert began, any pain or discomfort seemed to disappear for him. The familiar and comforting music of his favorite band served as a natural analgesic. He just smiled the whole time and even danced.

At one point in the concert, the people in front of us stood up on their chairs, dancing away. Since we could no longer see the band, Scott decided to get up on his chair too! "What are you doing, Scott? Come down!" But instead of listening to me and coming down, he reached down for my hand, and gently pulled, suggesting that I stand too! *Who am I to ruin this moment for him? Stand up, Peggy! Dance with him!* I allowed him to gently pull me up, and for just one song, we danced on our chairs, laughing and singing the lyrics to "Foolish Heart." He was so happy. I looked over at my friends who had given us the tickets, and they radiated happiness! My sense was that they were beaming with happiness and pride because they were responsible for this moment.

At the end of the concert, Scott clutched his back as we were herded with hundreds of other fans through a tunnel on a walk back to our car that seemed to last for miles. Only the pure adrenaline high of seeing his favorite band partially masked Scott's pain. That night, it was almost as if he didn't have cancer.

When Scott felt well, and even when he didn't, he was active. He attended as many concerts as he could, including Big Head Todd and the Monsters, Blues Traveler, The Allman Brothers Band, and Crosby, Stills, and Nash. He went roller blading and bike riding. On one particular ride with my mom and dad along the Delaware and Raritan Canal, he was so full of energy that he stayed in front the whole time. The path along the canal stretched wide enough across for two bikes to ride side by side. It was flat and straight. At one point, Scott turned to my dad.

"Wanna race?" he asked. My dad looked over at him.

"You're on!" They took off, pedaling with all their might. My mother and I kept up our leisurely pace, as the two of them became smaller and smaller in our view. They looked and sounded like two elementary-school-aged boys in competition. Finally, they stopped. Although we couldn't see who won, we knew it was Scott, as both of his arms went up in the air in victory.

That summer, five months after Scott's diagnosis of cancer, we continued with our wedding plans, including our engagement party. One sunny Saturday, my parents' deck was filled with people—from friends I'd known more than twenty years to new ones we'd met since Scott was diagnosed, including Kevin, his hospital roommate. As engagement parties go, it was huge. My father had agreed we could invite more than half our wedding guest list. Like me, he, too, worried Scott might die before the wedding.

But that day, we pushed all such thoughts aside. I felt like a princess, even though I was dressed in a University of Vermont sweatshirt and shorts. Scott was clean-shaven and handsome. The event kicked off a happy August.

We visited the pastor of my parish. Since we were living together, we weren't allowed to attend the traditional Catholic Pre-Cana classes with other couples. Instead, we had to attend pre-marriage counseling as a couple with the monsignor. During our first session, the monsignor asked us why we love each other. He turned to Scott first. "Scott, why do you love Peggy?" he asked. "Why do you want to marry her?" While Scott was a wonderful man, he rarely got deep or emotional. I wondered what he was going to say. The question took him by surprise. He looked at me and put his hand on my knee. He paused for a moment, gathering his thoughts, and I held my breath. My lips quivered and tears streamed down my face.

"I love her because . . . I love her because she's everything to me. She's smart. She's funny. She has so much love. She cares deeply for people. She cares deeply for me." He swallowed. "She makes me feel alive." It physically hurt to hear Scott say why he loved me because I feared that our time may be coming to an end.

Then it was my turn. I had so much to say, but the words were not coming out. I cried as I looked at him, handsome as ever with his bald head. My crying turned to sobbing as I closed my eyes and my shoulders shook with each sob. There was concern in Scott's eyes, a look of worry about how I was handling his illness. Those feelings went unspoken. They were something we never discussed. We never talked about his illness, how he was feeling, and how I was coping. I didn't want to bring that into the conversation now, even though losing him was always on my mind, despite my efforts to push those thoughts aside. I stopped crying just long enough to speak through my tears. I had to say something.

"I love Scott because he is so loving. He is kind, thoughtful, smart, and funny. I love how he makes me laugh. I love how he makes me feel special. I love watching him interact with other people, making them feel special. I love his positive attitude. I love his strength. I just love him."

While Scott respected my religion and my desire to be married in a Catholic church, he was agnostic. Pragmatic and concrete, he could not understand or believe what he could not see or touch. When he said he didn't believe in God and thought of the Bible as a collection of short stories, I was sure the monsignor would not marry us. We got a pass, though, probably because Scott had cancer and his bald head was like holding a big sign that read, "I'm fighting for my life."

We visited the DJ we had chosen for our wedding to go over what kind of music and what general "vibe" we wanted. As soon as the DJ saw Scott's bald head, I could tell that he knew that Scott was sick. He had that look of sympathy that was becoming familiar to me. Scott must have sensed it too, because he said, "Don't worry, man. I've got cancer, but I'm OK. I'm beating it, and I feel great!"

We told the DJ that we wanted the most upbeat songs from the 70s and 80s that would inspire people to dance. This was to be a celebration of not just our marriage, but Scott's triumph over cancer. As we sat down and went through all our song choices, I tried hard to believe that we would be celebrating both. I tried hard to push away the thoughts that I would be alone and celebrating neither.

Knowing that wedding planning would keep us busy, Scott and I had been planning a long weekend in Mystic, Connecticut, and Newport, Rhode Island. We decided to honor our plans, no matter what. On our way to Mystic, we stopped for an appointment with his oncologist to go over the details of his bone marrow transplant. Meanwhile, in the waiting room, I read all the brochures and pamphlets for which I'd sent away to help us plan our honeymoon. My body was in the doctor's office, but in my mind's eye, I was driving the Pacific Coast Highway on Route 1 in California.

Eventually, Scott emerged from the doctor's office.

"How'd it go?" I asked. It bothered me that he had to meet with the doctor without me. He also was undergoing some kind of testing at which I could not be present.

"I don't want to talk about it," he said. "Let's just go." So we walked in silence down the hospital corridor. I couldn't wait to get out of there. We got to the parking lot, and there was his Celica winking at us.

We got in the car, and I waited for him to say something, anything.

Scott loved to talk when things were lighthearted and jovial. Then he was the life of the party. Serious stuff was not his thing, and this was serious stuff, really serious stuff, stuff that *I* needed to talk about. But I didn't want to push. I figured that over the course of the next few days together, he would give me bits and pieces so I could understand what was going on.

All he could tell me was that he would be in the hospital for a long time for his bone marrow transplant. I didn't even want to ask him how long. I didn't want to know. The thought of being without him again made me very sad.

❄ ❄ ❄

We drove all the way from the hospital in Westchester, New York to Mystic, Connecticut without stopping and barely talking. It was a beautiful sunny day with low humidity—the kind of day I knew wouldn't make Scott feel sick or tire him too much. In Mystic, we parked the car on the street and walked along the shoreline, admiring the boats. We stopped for lunch at Mystic Pizza, made famous by the movie starring Julia Roberts. The pizzeria turned out to be bland, unexciting—nothing like the place in the movie. I felt disappointed. But maybe that was simply the way I was feeling that day.

As we ate, I started crying. I loved every moment with Scott but was anticipating missing him when he went in for his transplant. I had already lived through that pain and loneliness during his month-long first round of treatment. Since he'd been discharged from the hospital in April, we had enjoyed our time together at home. I knew I'd be with him every day at the hospital during the transplant, but it wouldn't be the same.

"What's wrong, Peg?" he asked.

"I'm going to miss you," I replied. He clammed up.

"I don't want to talk about that," he said. As much as I wanted to talk to Scott about how sad and scared I was, I had to respect his wishes. After all, it was his life. He was the sick one. But the silence left me feeling even more lonely and, actually, quite angry at him. I knew we were different in terms of talking about and processing emotions, but I resented him for not meeting me halfway. He shut me down by simply refusing to hear anything about my feelings and fears. It hurt. I was mad and then found myself not being able to talk about anything. When he tried to make light conversation, I couldn't say anything. I wanted him to know how much it pained me that he wouldn't listen to how I felt. How much I cared about him. How lonely I was going to be without him while he was in the hospital. How terrified I was of losing him.

After Scott and I left Mystic Pizza, we aimlessly strolled along the sidewalk in and out of quaint boutiques. Mostly, we walked in silence. I was still feeling quite sad and hurt and not up to talking. As we walked in to one small women's boutique, Scott told me to take my time; he'd meet me outside. I spent a couple minutes browsing the beautiful clothing, trying to snap out of my sadness so that we could enjoy this time together.

When I came outside, I saw a parked car along the sidewalk. Scott was leaning into the opened car window, laughing. *Who the heck does he know here?* I quickly went over to see what was going on. It was the Nardones! They were vacationing in Mystic too! Jody was the dear friend Scott and I had gone to see perform at the Bernards Inn the night before I left for Colorado. Jody and Scott had become close friends, and now we shared a connection that none of us wanted. Jody's father was in the midst of cancer treatment, just like Scott. It warmed and broke my heart to see these two jovial men, laughing their heads off during a time when they were both fighting for their lives. In that moment, I knew what was important. Love.

Seeing the Nardone family and feeling their love for each other, it occurred to me that Scott could not tolerate talking about his illness because he loved me so much. I came to the realization that he was in so much pain already that he simply could not bear to think about my emotional pain. I felt a sense of relief and sweetness toward him when I thought of the situation that way, which I really believed to be true. He cared about me so deeply that he could not tolerate listening to my pain. I accepted this lovingly and resolved to find people who could tolerate listening to my emotional distress, including my mother, my father, and my dear friends Kristen, Nancy, Jeriann, Ali, Jennifer, and Amy.

I felt better just knowing that I could talk to these special people about my worries and fears. Caregivers need support, too. I was used to getting all my nurturance from Scott, but this was one area where he simply could not provide the care I needed and that had to be OK.

Scott slept most of the way on our drive from Mystic to Newport. When we got there, he still felt tired, so I helped him into the canopy bed at our charming bed-and-breakfast inn. I was surprised that our room had two floors. We quickly explored our beautiful accommodations, but Scott was too tired to enjoy or appreciate it. All he wanted to do was lie down. Immediately, he dozed off. I walked through the French doors leading from the bedroom onto our balcony and looked out over the harbor. In the distance was Newport Bridge, its lights glistening in the darkening blue sky. Oh, how I wished he was standing by my side taking in this gorgeous view.

As Scott slumbered soundly, I put on a jacket, kissed his forehead, and left to walk around the town. I left him a note saying I'd be back soon. I walked toward the pier, where I saw a couple holding hands. They looked to be in their seventies. I fantasized that they were there to celebrate their fiftieth wedding anniversary. A wave of sadness overcame me. Scott and I had pushed our wedding date back to June 6, 1995 in the hope he'd be finished with his treatment by then. Suddenly, I thought that June was too far away. My fears took over and seemed uncontrollable, as I allowed myself to think about him dying before our wedding. I wanted to be like that older couple, holding hands and enjoying each other's company in this romantic spot. I became intensely jealous of them. Everywhere I walked, people, noise, and laughter surrounded me. Who could possibly imagine that I was out by myself because my fiancé was sick with cancer and sleeping on the canopy bed? I felt completely alone.

When I got back to the room, Scott was awake and said he felt better, so we took a sunset cruise. We held hands and, in silence, enjoyed the colors of the sun setting. If he didn't feel well, he didn't show it.

This reprieve didn't last long.

When we returned to our room, Scott felt sick again. I was sure he had a fever, but we didn't have a thermometer. As night fell and we fretted, the outdoor sounds wafted into our room. People were gathering, listening to music, laughing.

Scott refused to go to the emergency room. All he wanted to do was sleep. I stood at the balcony, alternating between gazing at the ocean and checking on Scott. I just let him sleep. He looked peaceful. I prayed he was not in discomfort or pain when he slept. I knew he would protest, but as I slipped into bed beside him, I vowed we would leave in the morning.

When he woke up feeling better, he didn't want to go home.

"I decided I wanted to stay," he said.

"I don't think it's a good idea," I replied. "You were so sick last night. I think you have a fever. We need to go home."

"No. Really. I'm fine. I want to stay. We *are* staying." So we went to breakfast in the Harbor Room; toured Hammersmith Farm, a Victorian mansion, and the wedding reception location for John F. Kennedy and Jacqueline Bouvier; took a driving tour on Ocean Avenue to see the private mansions; and parked at The Breakers and toured the Cliff Walk behind the other mansions. At a cliff wall, we stopped, held hands, and gazed at the ocean for a while. I still had a pit in my stomach and couldn't stop thinking that would be the last time we'd look out at the ocean together. So I savored the moment and squeezed Scott's hand a little tighter.

# Death's Door

### August 29, 1994

The day after we returned home, I went to work in the morning. Scott said he felt well, but I told him to call the doctor anyway. He went to see his doctor, and his oncologist sent him home with antibiotics. When I got home from work, he still wasn't feeling well, so we snuggled in bed, napped, and watched television.

The next day, when I got home from work, Scott still wasn't feeling well. "Oh, sweetie. What can I do for you? You need to eat something. Maybe you will feel a little bit better if you eat something,"

"I don't have much of an appetite," he said, "but maybe I can get some soup down."

We didn't have any soup, so I said I would go out to get some. "I don't want to leave you alone, though. Do you think you'll be OK if I go out and get it? Should I ask your mom to get it while I stay with you?"

"I'll be OK," he replied. "I'll just rest here until you get back. Don't worry. I'll be fine."

I went out quickly to get the soup, feeling uneasy and worrying about him the whole time. I was only gone fifteen minutes, but it felt much longer.

By the time I returned, he was in the bathroom vomiting. As soon as I walked in the door, I heard him throwing up. Dropping the grocery bag on the floor, I ran to him. "Scott! Oh, Scott!" He was sweating and shaking. I helped him wipe his face and held him by the shoulder and elbow as I guided him to the bed. "Lay down. Let me get a thermometer," I said. "You feel so warm, and you're sweating."

"That's because it's hot in here!" he said. "I feel much better now." He always said he felt better after he threw up.

"I'm taking your temperature anyway." Getting the thermometer from the bathroom, I quickly came back and placed it in his mouth and sat on our bed next to him until I thought the reading was done. I slowly took it out of his mouth. 103. *I knew it. Damn!*

"I'm calling the hospital," I said in a panic. He did not protest. He just lay there, pale and shaking. I went and got the doctor's number and called from the phone attached to the wall in the hallway. As I picked up the phone, I looked at the plaque I made: Peggy and Scott. I dialed the number.

"Oncology," the woman answered. *Oh how I hate that word.*

"This is Peggy Doherty. My fiancé Scott Unger is a patient there. He's got a fever of 103, and he's vomiting and shaking." I tried hard to remain calm and not let my voice shake. I did not want Scott to hear that.

"Let me get his chart," the nurse said. She put me on hold and quickly returned. "I see he was just here yesterday with a fever. Has he been taking the antibiotics?"

I don't know. "Scott, have you been taking the antibiotics?" I could hear a faint, "Yes." "Yes, he has," I told the nurse.

"Bring him in right away," she said.

I quickly hung up the phone. As I began packing some things for both of us, I explained to him that the nurse said to bring him to the emergency room. He watched me pack.

"I don't need all that stuff. Don't pack all those shorts and underwear. I don't need them. I'm sure they'll send me home, just like they did yesterday." I so badly wanted to believe this, but I didn't. He was too sick.

Scott was admitted. For days, the doctors didn't know what was wrong. I worked half-days so I could be with him the rest of the time. During the few hours I was not there, he would often call me, just to say he loved me. It meant so much to me that I meant so much to him.

For the next week, the doctors could not figure out the problem. They told us that they couldn't find any signs of cancer. They said he might have an infection or be reacting to the medication. I had trouble believing this. I thought they were trying to protect us from the awful news that the cancer had returned.

After Scott had been there for three days, I thought it would be nice for him to see some pictures and the cards that were coming for him in the mail. I began to post them to his cork bulletin board. "I brought some pictures from home for you," I said happily.

"Don't put those up. I'm not staying here. I'll be going home any day now." I knew it was important for him to keep this mentality, so I immediately took them down.

"How about I just put this one here, right by your bed, so when I'm not here, you can still see me." Then I took out the photo of me that he had placed on the bulletin board when he first began his treatment. I still didn't know where that picture came from. He acquiesced and allowed me to place the photo of me near him. He smiled, and I squeezed his hand.

The moment was interrupted by the doctor entering the room.

Without wasting any time, he abruptly delivered the bad news. "Scott, the cancer has returned."

We were still holding hands. I could feel Scott squeezing my hand hard, then harder. I don't think he had any awareness of how tightly he held my hand. With this news, I felt like I was going to faint. I had difficulty hearing the doctor's words, but I was able to understand that the cancer was now in his kidneys and liver.

Bravely, Scott asked, "What does this mean?"

"Well," the doctor said, "we're going to start you back on chemotherapy right away. And because your kidneys are not functioning properly, you will also start dialysis right away."

❄ ❄ ❄

I just wanted to cry. I wanted to break down and cry. Had I been alone, I would have. But I could not do that in front of Scott. I needed to be strong for him.

"You are going to get through this, honey. You are so strong. You are going to get through this." I leaned over and kissed his forehead, mustering every ounce of energy not to cry.

He said stoically, "I know. I know." Then he added quietly, "I'm just tired of this." I realized then that throughout this whole awful experience, that was his only complaint. Never, "Why me?" or "This is not fair." Just a quiet, "I'm tired of this." My heart broke for him.

Scott suggested that I go home. "It's been a long day, and you've been here with me nonstop while you've still got to work." Normally, I would have protested and stayed longer, but I could sense that I was nearing exhaustion. I was dizzy and nauseous. If I was not careful, I was going to need to be hospitalized too. I gathered up my things, and I kissed him on the cheek.

"I'll be back in the morning," I said.

With his eyes closed, he said, "I'm looking forward to it. I love you."

"I love you, too." I drove home in the dark. As it was one o'clock in the morning when I arrived home, my parents were sleeping. I quietly crawled in my bed and quickly fell asleep.

Scott began his chemotherapy the next morning. His mother stayed with him all day and told me to rest. I was grateful, as I was already feeling so weak, tired, and dizzy. She told me Scott was so exhausted that his mouth could not form words to speak to me over the phone. I asked her to tell him that I loved him.

"I will." Speaking for him, she added, "He loves you, too."

Since my return from Colorado, that was the first day Scott and I didn't see or talk to each other. It broke my heart. I was also upset that I couldn't get the ugly cancer images out of my head: The dry creases of his lips were black with blood. His eyes looked yellow.

After Scott had been in the hospital about two weeks, I arrived one day with my parents for a long visit on a Saturday. We bumped into Scott's father in the parking lot. He didn't smile upon greeting us.

"I've got some bad news," he said, motioning for us to step out of the lot and onto the grass under a tree. "We spoke to the doctor." He paused for a moment. "The doctor said that Scott's condition couldn't be worse. He has about a week to live."

"What?" I asked. I heard him, but it couldn't be true. Scott had been improving. He was going to live.

"Are they sure? How can they know?" I asked, my lips quivering. There was no need for discussing Scott's condition any further. Mr. Unger was in so much pain. I did not want to make him say anything more. I could see and feel that it was a knife in his heart. His only son was dying. Still, I wanted to hold on to hope.

Mr. Unger turned and walked away quietly.

"See you later," he said, his voice barely a whisper. My mother put her hands on my shoulders, turned me toward her, and hugged me with all her might. I cried harder than I have ever cried in my life. But I was not ready to let go of hope. I had tried so hard to believe that Scott was going to be that one medical miracle. I was not ready to give up. We left the parking lot and walked into the hospital toward Scott's room in silence. *How can this be happening? Just two weeks ago we were picking out our wedding music. Should I let his friends know so they can visit before he dies? Or hang onto the hope he wasn't going to die and let them visit him at home?*

When Mom and I stepped off the elevator, Scott's sister Gretchen was there. She hugged me tightly.

"Thanks for giving Scott a beautiful summer, Peg," she said. I just stared at her, still refusing to acquiesce. If anyone could beat this cancer, it was Scott. I believed in miracles. So I silently asked for a miracle for Scott and prayed for strength for myself.

The next sight I saw in Scott's room unnerved me. Six strong men were restraining him as he struggled to pull the dialysis tube out of his neck, a move that would have killed him. He wanted to get out of bed and clearly did not understand what was happening to him. He was panicked, frightened, and those men were trying to save him from himself.

Finally, he calmed down. They motioned for me to enter. I nodded to the male aide of the day sitting in a corner near the window in the shadows. Someone monitored Scott twenty-four hours a day, so we never had privacy. I thought the presence of the monitor would feel intrusive.

Actually, I felt safer and less alone in the sterile darkness of the room. I thought of the aide as Scott's protector.

I decided that I had to tell Chris, his best buddy. I knew he would want to know. I called his home, and his mother answered the phone. "Chris is in Washington, DC. What's the matter, dear? You're scaring me!" I was crying. She knew that Scott was in the hospital, as he was Chris's best friend, and she had known Scott since he was a little boy. She began to cry too.

"The doctors say that Scott does not have very long to live. I thought Chris would want to know," I somehow managed to say through my tears.

"I will tell him right away," she said. "I know he wants to be there. He's going to be there. Thank you for calling," and we both hung up, both still crying.

His night nurse that shift was a strong, big, very friendly man. He spoke kindly to Scott and gave him the respect he deserved. He even got me a lounge chair to sleep on. I slept next to Scott and held his hand all night, trying not to touch his restraint. He was still confused and often thrashed around, banging his restraints against his bed. My sweet Scott, who was always gentle, was angry and aggressive. I looked at him but did not see him. I saw the cancer taking over him. Everything that touched his body made him bleed.

"Get me out of here, Peggy!" he screamed in the middle of the night. The words broke my heart. I couldn't do anything to get him out.

News quickly spread that Scott's condition had deteriorated and that he did not have much time to live. That Sunday, a steady stream of visitors came and went: my mother, my father, my two brothers, my sister, my sister's husband, Scott's mother, Scott's father, Scott's sisters and their partners, and Chris.

It hurt to see them. The sadness in my father's eyes seared me most of all. After everyone left, it was quiet again. I walked into the room. Scott appeared exhausted.

"Here is your lovely fiancée, Peggy," his night nurse said.

"Congratulations," he said.

"No, dear," I replied. "We're getting married. *You* are my fiancé."

"Are you proud?" he asked. I choked up and nodded.

The next day, Scott's nurse needed to wash him. Scott was so calm that his nurse was able to remove the restraints from his hands. When he did, the look of satisfaction and relief on Scott's face made me cry.

"It's fine for Peggy to stay and help you," he told the nurse. I was honored he was allowing me to witness and participate in an activity of pure vulnerability. When he was washed up, he chose his short-sleeved, orange Ralph Lauren polo shirt to wear. He tried to talk, but much of what he said did not make sense.

"Our wedding is in a couple of hours," he told me. "I'll see you there."

"Sweetie, I won't be there in a few hours," I replied. "I'll be there in a few months."

"I want to go home now," he said. He paused. "Please put on the Sports Channel." I complied, happy he had the energy to watch anything.

Despite the illness, the tubes, the medications, the doctors and nurses, and the sterility of the room, bits of Scott's personality were able to shine through, including his desire to be intimate.

"Want to go upstairs with me?" he asked, winking. When Chris arrived, Scott greeted him.

"You're the man!" Scott said, as he had dozens of times when Chris visited our apartment. "Hey, will you put on the Allman Brothers CD?" Chris complied. "Good tunes," Scott murmured as he listed to the album.

He wanted to get up to use the bathroom, but he still wasn't allowed out of bed. I had to repeatedly tell him that he was hooked up to a tube that allowed him to urinate while lying in bed.

"Is that the truth?" he asked the nurse.

"Yes, she's telling the truth," he replied. Scott smiled weakly.

"I know," he said. "I love her. I love her." He was so happy, listening to the Allman Brothers, bopping his head to the music. As nighttime neared, Chris said he was planning on spending the night. I relinquished my bedside chair to him and went down the hall to the lounge to sleep there. The two best friends needed time together, and I needed rest.

When I came in to see Scott the next morning at 7:00, he looked great. His mouth was clean. His restraints were off. He extended a hand, touched my cheek, and tried to pull me closer to kiss him on the lips. I froze, fearful that kissing him on the lips would make him sicker because of his compromised immune system.

"For now, I have to kiss you on the cheek," I said, after which he puckered his lips and tried hard to kiss my lips. It killed me not to kiss him. Suddenly, he got a nosebleed that would not stop.

"I want to go home," he said. "I want to go home."

"Soon, Scott," I replied. "Soon, honey, when you're better."

"Now," he said.

"Soon." He looked up at me.

"I hope so. I'm trying." Then he fell asleep. Minutes later, he awakened with a start.

"Peg!" he yelled out in a panic.

"I'm right here," I said. "I'm right here with you."

I had some more difficult phone calls to make. That day, I was supposed to have started my doctoral program at Pace University. Instead, I called up the program director to let her know what was going on in my life, and that I would not be able to attend. She was very caring and compassionate. "Don't worry, dear," Dr. Mowder said. "We will hold your spot. You are welcome to enter the program whenever you're ready." That upset Scott. He knew how hard I'd worked to get in and how I'd been planning this for years. It didn't matter anymore. It could wait. I needed to be with him every minute. Then I had to make another call to my employer.

"Dr. Jack, I need to take a leave of absence. "Scott is really sick, and they don't expect him to live much longer." I had cried so much, that I was able to utter these words without crying. Dr. Jack was a kind and compassionate child psychiatrist. I was not surprised that he was so understanding of my situation.

"Your job is waiting for you whenever you want to return. We love you, Peggy. Everyone here sends their love, to you and Scott."

The next day, Scott was getting dialysis when I entered. He was able to stay still, but I was afraid he'd try to pull the tube out of his neck again. I couldn't watch. I moved to sit on the other side of him, so I didn't have to see the wide tube with blood. To my surprise, he started talking about sex. I couldn't make out everything he was saying, but he had that look in his eye.

"Are we going to make kids?" he asked.

"Of course. After we get married, we certainly are." Later in the day, although he was not making sense, he was talking well. He tried to reason his way out of his restraints, first asking for scissors, then a knife, then the toolbox out of his car so he could cut the strap to free his hands. When my mom arrived, he made silly faces and shifted his gaze slyly from one of us to the other. I never imagined I could be so happy just to hear him talk. He was coming back from the brink of death.

Scott continued to get better. He was allowed to eat and drink what he wanted and at one time ordered pizza.

"Make it four slices," he told the nurse. "One for Peg, one for Chris, one for me, one for you."

When I spent the night, I usually didn't get any sleep, so I went home to rest before coming back. Whenever I couldn't be there overnight, my parents were there together or taking turns. During the day, his parents, siblings, or friends were always at his side. Scott was never alone. I was grateful to have my parents with him and to get full, detailed reports. It seemed strange to get the report from my father that Scott was able to get out of bed, sit in a chair, and use the toilet. We were celebrating his being able to use the toilet.

During this time, Scott showed his tender side. He told his nurses and doctors that he loved me and that he asked me to be his wife. One time when just my father and I were in the room, he looked solemnly at my dad.

"I love your daughter," he said, very seriously. He looked around at the cards and gifts surrounding him. "There is so much love in this room." Though Scott was a loving person, he never talked like that, and I was scared to think of what the sudden change could mean. One day his doctor came in and declared Scott had improved a lot in just a few days.

"Yeah," Scott said, "I was at death's door."

"We don't like to say that word around here," the doctor said.

"What, door?" Scott quipped. He pointed to his nurse. "Don, he's my savior." Then he pointed to his monitor, Dale. "And this guy here," he said, squeezing Dale's hand. "Everybody, the whole team, is great and helped me to get better. There is no 'I' in T-E-A-M."

Yet Scott had trouble sleeping. He'd often roll toward me at night and just look at me. We tried to hold hands, but it was difficult to do that through the metal bars on the side of his bed. Fearful he would roll out of bed if I took the bars down, I let them be.

At 3:00 a.m. one day, a doctor gently roused Scott so he could remove the catheter for dialysis from Scott's neck. Scott made him laugh by wiggling his ears. I stayed with him until 4:00 a.m. and then got my mother from the lounge so I could get some sleep. Once I left and my mother was next to him, he woke up and kept asking for me. He was so persistent that my mother came to get me. He only wanted me.

My parents went through so much, coming with me to the hospital, sleeping in the recliner next to Scott, loving him like he was their own son. My mother even started donating platelets. Hers didn't go directly to Scott, but it touched me that she was literally giving her physical self away. I worried, though, that the stress was taking a toll on both my parents. I was young. The lack of sleep was making me physically ill. It must have been doing the same to them, but they never showed it.

One morning when I hadn't spent the night, Scott called me at six o'clock. I asked him why he was calling me so early when I would be there in just a few hours.

"Peg, I just want you to make a list of everyone you know who has died," he said.

"Why, sweetheart?"

"I'm seeing them," he said, "but I don't know who all of them are." A shiver racked my body.

"Where have you been?" Scott asked me, the second I walked into his room. I was a half hour later than I'd told him I would arrive because I'd I stopped at our apartment in Chatham to get his robe at his request.

"Did you bring the list?" he asked. He'd remembered.

"No, I didn't get a chance."

"Peg," he said.

"Yes?"

"I changed my mind, after all." I reached out and touched his forehead.

"About what?"

"There is a God," he said. While I was comforted that he'd changed his mind, I was also terrified. *What happened? Did he go to 'the other side'? Did he see 'the light'?* Anything I could come up with made me think that he was closer to death.

The big news of that day was that his urine and dialysis catheters were removed. He was finally permitted to get up and walk. He celebrated by inviting everyone to walk the halls with him. He walked and walked and walked in his white, belted, terry cloth robe, smiling and waving to every patient, nurse, and doctor along the way.

He asked me to spend every night with him, but I was frail and not eating. I would try to eat breakfast with my parents in the coffee shop downstairs, try to force cereal down my throat. But every bite made me feel sick. I knew I needed energy. I was dizzy all the time and physically exhausted from spending night after night at his bedside. My attention was fused to him. I followed his every move. It got to the point where when he vomited, I vomited.

One morning at 7:00, I was awakened by a terrible crashing sound. *Holy crap! Scott tried to climb over his bed rail!* I looked over to see that he had crashed against the hard floor as all his tubes were pulled out of him. I jumped up, getting out of bed faster than I ever have in my life.

"Scott! Scott! Oh, what did you do? Scott!" I panicked, as he lay there, helpless, with all of these tubes hanging around him. "Nurse! He needs help! Help!"

Very quickly, a nurse came in. Then another. *Thank God.* They slowly lifted him up from the floor, each woman placing her hand under his arm to lift him.

"I'm sorry," Scott said. "I just wanted to get out of bed." I realized that he was so confused, that he did not know that he was attached to so many tubes. One nurse put down the metal guardrail so that he could get back in, and slowly and gently, they both guided him back into the bed. Scott gave out a sigh.

"Ahh," I could hear, ever so softly.

As soon as I realized that Scott was OK, I felt as though I was about to faint. I leaned against the bed before hitting the floor. "What happened?" I asked, confused. *Why am I on the floor?*

"You fainted, my dear," the sweet Irish nurse Eileen said. "Let's get you up on the bed." This was a rare occasion when Scott did not have a roommate, and the bed on the other side of the room was empty. This is where I had slept the night before.

I felt funny. I had a whooshing sound in my ears. My vision was not clear, and I felt confused. *What's going on? What's happening to me?* A nurse sensed my panic and comforted me. "You must be exhausted, dear. Peggy, right? I see you here every day, here with your fiancé, Scott." She glanced over at Scott, and he winked at her.

The nurses then had to care for me, taking my pulse and blood pressure. "Don't worry, my dear. We'll take care of you. You're going to be just fine. You're in the right place." Then she joked, "And we won't even charge you." I managed to muster a smile. My smile quickly disappeared when I looked over at Scott. I saw his face, eyes wide with fear. He was concerned for me.

That fainting was a sign that I needed to take better care of myself. *How can I take care of Scott if I am sick, too? How can I have him worrying about ME?*

After that, I regularly rotated at night with my mother and father. I just could not do it by myself no matter how much that reality saddened me. I was always the only one he wanted. I was there every day and night, but when I felt as though I was nearing exhaustion, I would sleep on the sofa in the lounge at the end of the hall and one of my parents would sleep in a lounge chair next to Scott.

Every morning, I comforted myself with a simple ritual: before visiting Scott, I bought a cup of hazelnut coffee in the cafeteria. The aroma permeated his hospital room and made it less sterile, more like home. I liked the warmth from the cup, the taste, the predictable availability during every one of the unpredictable, anxiety-provoking days. Scott knew how much that cup of coffee meant to me, and he encouraged me to stretch my legs and go down the several flights to the cafeteria to get it or ask someone to get it for me when he didn't want me to leave his side.

The days were filled with ups and downs, mostly downs. Scott either had a fever, or vomited, or couldn't stop shaking. He had trouble speaking, and when he did speak, he often didn't make sense. One time he woke up abruptly.

"Peg, what are we going to do with all the extra sandwiches?" he asked. In spite of being confused and nonsensical, though, he regularly introduced me whenever someone new walked into the room.

"Meet my future wife," he said, glancing at me since he had trouble pointing with his arm. We played his favorite music at all times, as this seemed to have a soothing effect. He closed his eyes and gently bopped his head to the sounds of the Allman Brothers and the Grateful Dead.

Miraculously, Scott started feeling better and more energized. He was allowed to eat anything he wanted, which meant Wendy's hamburgers and French fries. He used his newfound energy to engage in what little activity he could—moving from the bed to his chair, walking to the bathroom in his room, strolling a few rooms down to the lounge, and on a really good morning, venturing downstairs to the cafeteria for breakfast.

On the afternoon of Friday, October 7, 1994, I was alone with Scott in his room. For the first time, the protector was not there. I knew Scott did not want to hear about how his illness was having an effect on me. It was too much for him. Too painful. But I could not stop the tears.

"I just miss you so much!" I cried. "I know I see you every day, but I miss being with you at home. I miss our life at home." I could not help it, and my cry turned into a sob. I put my head down and covered my face with both of my hands.

After I had composed myself somewhat and was once again able to speak, I said quietly, "I can't wait for you to come home."

"Don't worry," he said. "I'll be home before you know it." I wanted to tell him I was afraid of losing him and how lonely I'd be without him. I wanted to know what he wanted me to do if he died. *Do you want me to remain single? Is there some way you want to communicate with me? Will you come to me in my dreams? Through music? Are you scared? What do you want me to do?* But I could not ask these questions or tell him how I felt. He still never wanted to talk about any such subject. We never talked about his illness. We never talked about death.

By Sunday, October 9, I had reached pure exhaustion. I was concerned I could not think, sleep, or eat. I needed a break from sleeping on the hospital floor and chair. So I slept at my parents' house and just kept sleeping and sleeping. I woke up, groggy—still exhausted. I decided not to visit, figuring one day away from the hospital would make me feel human again and give me the stamina to keep going. I called Scott to let him know I was not coming. I assured him that I would be there first thing in the morning. Although he was speaking almost unintelligibly during our conversation, he managed to say one thing very clearly: "I'm looking forward to it."

Since I did not visit that day, I asked some of his friends to visit so he wouldn't be alone. Knowing he had company, my mother took me to the mall to buy Scott a present—the first time I'd been in public in seven weeks. It felt strange to be around people. People who were not visiting sick loved ones. I didn't have the energy to walk far.

"Mom, can you just park here? Then we can just walk into Macy's and get something." My mother parked as close to the door as she could, and we walked a short distance into Macy's. I found something perfect for Scott in the men's department—a pair of New York Rangers silk boxer shorts in the hope the very personal gift would cheer him up when I arrived the next morning. I couldn't wait to give it to him!

When I arrived at the hospital on Monday, October 10, three nurses were in Scott's room. They were about to put him on a ventilator to help him breathe since his heart was beating so fast.

"We have to do something. Otherwise, he'll go into cardiac arrest," the doctor told me. "He's been asking for you this morning." I approached the bed and handed Scott the silk boxers. He tried to smile.

"Talk to him now, honey," one of the nurses said. "Soon he won't be able to talk." He asked for his wallet, so his sister Jill went to his closet to get it. He took out some money and handed it to me.

"This is for the operation," he said, referring to the intubation. I assumed he was joking, simply because he was always looking for an opportunity to make a joke. But I could not laugh. I could not even smile. Then I thought, *He's not joking. He's delirious. He does not understand what is happening to him.*

As soon as Scott's parents, my parents, and I were all together, a doctor came by and explained our options to us: We could put him on the ventilator and dialysis and give him a high dose of chemotherapy, but he would suffer and the chances of the cancer going away were very, very small to nonexistent. They had tried everything. The cancer was still spreading. We had another choice: give him morphine, make him comfortable, and let him go. After the morphine began, Scott would live for thirty-six to forty-eight hours.

We chose to let him go. *Why, oh why, did we have to make that awful decision?*

While he could still speak, Scott and I just told each other how much we loved each other. I didn't know how much he knew about what was happening. I didn't have any idea what he was thinking, but I was afraid he knew something awful was happening.

"Sorry," he said to me. "Sorry." What was he apologizing for? Loving me? Leaving me? Being sick? There was nothing to be sorry for.

I watched and watched and watched him. What if they were wrong, and instead of thirty-six hours, he was only alive for one hour? At first, he had an oxygen mask that he hated and kept taking off. Slowly, he stopped moving and entered a deep sleep. Still, I watched. I was afraid he would die the moment I took my eyes off of him. I worried he would die if I left the room, and I *had* to be there when he died.

I was afraid to go to the bathroom, afraid to close my eyes. I stayed awake all night in a chair next to him, trying to get as physically close to him as I could. What I really wanted was to get in that hospital bed and hold him tight and not let go, as if my love and grip would save him.

On the morning of Tuesday, October 11, 1994, Scott's breathing slowed down. Later in the afternoon, it was even slower. One by one, all his nurses came into his room after their shifts were over. They came to say goodbye.

Chris arrived around 7:30 p.m. I had not called him. I felt as though I put him through enough the last time the doctors told us that Scott was going to die soon. Somehow, he knew that he should be there. When he walked in, we were all sitting around Scott, holding and stroking him. Scott lay in his bed, with his head slightly elevated. His mother, his father, my mother, my father, Chris, and I all surrounded his body and touched him. I was at the right side of his head, holding his hand, leaning my face into his. I cried while still trying to hide my crying from him. I wanted to protect him. I did not want him to know how terribly heartbroken I was.

As the night went on, his breathing became more labored until he seemed to gasp at the end of each breath. His breathing was so slow and shallow that I had to watch the hair of his beard. With each breath, it moved ever so slightly. I whispered in his ear several times how much I loved him and how much I would miss him. I assured him he had been through enough, and now it was time to find peace.

Suddenly, his eyes opened up slightly. The hair on his neck that I'd been watching so closely pulsated irregularly. The time between the slight movement of his hair became longer and longer. Ten minutes after he opened his eyes, he took one big breath. His last breath felt like my last breath. I squeezed his hand tightly. At 10:33 p.m., he left his body ever so quietly.

"Oh, my sweetheart," I gasped. "Oh, my sweetheart. Oh, my sweetheart."

# The Chairlift

## October 11, 1994

*I* walked to the hallway, leaned against a wall, and fell to the floor. My mother and father pulled me back up and hugged and held me. Then I walked back into Scott's room to see him again. I told him I loved him, kissed his forehead, and held his hand. I could not feel him there anymore.

My mother and I drove home together. I pictured my father crying in his car, all by himself.

This awful confrontation with death frightened me. I wondered where Scott was. Where did he go? How could he be here one minute, and then gone, all while holding my hand? Life, and then no life, in an instant. I could not make sense of it. My mother slept in my room with me. I felt like a young child.

To me, October 12 always will be The Day After. The Day After Scott died. The Day After my future died. The Day After my heart died. The only thing that kept me from going crazy was a constant stream of visitors and phone calls.

Scott's mother called and wanted my approval for everything that was being planned for his funeral. I had only known Scott for three years, and we were not married. Yet I felt like a widow, so I was grateful to be considered in the plans to lay him to rest. His mother thanked me for everything I did for him. I did not need thanks. I only loved him as best as I could.

"He loved you, too, dear," she said. She meant well, but the words were a knife in my heart. It was hard to hear "love" in the past tense.

I remained terrified to be alone, day or night. Kristen flew in from graduate school in Arizona and arrived the next day. Sensing my fear, she stayed with me overnight in my room.

My excruciating pain was compounded by witnessing my father's grief. I know he was sad for me, but he also was feeling his own overwhelming loss. He loved Scott like a son. Normally, my father was always a happy man—unusually happy in fact, and a bit goofy too. He had this spirit about him that exuded joy, and my friends always commented how they felt it just being around him. I often imagined that he must have been such a wonderful gift to his psychiatry patients. I certainly knew how much he lifted me up. His warm smile could alleviate one's pain and sorrow, even on his own difficult days. And the beautiful thing about my father was that he was also not afraid to show sadness, sensitivity, and the capacity to feel.

But this was different. My father stopped smiling, and his face was unrecognizable. The absence of that smile affected me to my core. He had been so strong for me during Scott's illness, and I know it took a toll on him. Now he was showing his suffering; it scared me. I had never seen him like this before.

One night I woke up at one o'clock in the morning, needing to use the bathroom. I saw light peeking through the crack at the bottom of the door of my father's study. As I was in the hallway, I could hear him crying. Sobbing. While he was in front of me, he never allowed himself to fully experience his profound grief over Scott's death. I wanted to go to him, to comfort him. I decided to allow him to have his private moment and to talk to him about it in the morning.

"Dad, I heard you crying last night. You don't need to be strong for me anymore," I told him in the morning over a cup of coffee. Despite his grief, he maintained his usual routine of drinking coffee while reading the newspaper. My father placed his cup of coffee on an electric heater to keep it warm. Before sitting down, my father always spread out a bedsheet over the white couch and love seat. He was always afraid that the newspaper ink would rub off onto the furniture. I found this amusing, as no one ever went in to this room. No one would even notice. But he did it out of respect for my mother and the white furniture she had chosen for this room.

I continued, "You have been so incredibly strong for me throughout Scott's illness. It's OK to cry in front of me. It can't possibly make me feel any worse. I don't want to have to worry about you hiding your pain, crying when you're all alone."

"I loved him," my dad sobbed. "I loved him." He paused for a moment and added, "You sure know how to pick 'em!" We enjoyed a warm embrace of shared grief over the loss of a very special man.

I was sad for my loss. I was sad for my father's loss. But at the same time, I felt so grateful to have a loving, supportive father. His comforting presence made me feel as though I was going to survive.

Scott's wake was loud and filled with his friends from high school and college, all coming to pay their respects. There was laughter, as there should have been. Scott was a funny guy, and there were hundreds of funny stories to tell about him. My father told the one about Scott cutting the toe parts off the Rollerblades® that were too small for him. I talked about how every time someone asked Scott how he liked his coffee: "Black and strong, like my dog." We also joked about how Scott's idea of a good meal was what he called "chili-mac," mixing Hormel chili with Kraft macaroni and cheese! At times the stories and laughter got so loud, I felt bad for the other family with whom we were sharing the funeral home.

The next morning I couldn't wait to get into the funeral home: I wanted to see Scott's face one last time. I kneeled at the side of the casket and stroked his hair until his six pallbearers arrived. I could hardly breathe as all of them—Chris and Doug from his childhood, Tim and Bill from Northeastern University, and Charlie and Sean, his sisters' partners—lifted the casket and walked it to the hearse.

As we entered the church, I didn't expect it already would be full. I could not have walked down the aisle behind the casket at St. Patrick's Church in Chatham without Scott's sister Gretchen, who literally held me up. I could not even see through my tears as the organist played "Be Not Afraid," a song that used to make me cry during Mass when I was a child. I wanted to be walking down the aisle to marry the man I loved, not to bury his body. *How could this be? Just six weeks ago, we were vacationing in Newport. Eight weeks ago, we were celebrating our engagement at my parents' house. Seven months ago, he did not have a care in the world. Ten months ago, he got down on his knee and asked me to marry him.*

Somehow, I gave a eulogy for Scott, as did Gretchen, Chris, Tim, and my father.

Then came "The Irish Blessing," sung by Father Paddy: "May God give you for ev´ry storm a rainbow." As he sang, a ray of sunshine landed in front of my feet. With my gaze, I followed the beam to a window where

## The Chairlift

the vertical blinds had spread apart to let in the light. There was no wind to have moved the blinds. Gretchen leaned toward me.

"He's here," she whispered and squeezed my hand. We were both thinking the same thing.

Two of my friends from elementary school, Jody and Larry, both musicians, then sang our wedding song, "I Can See Clearly Now." It was fitting for this day, too. The suffering was over, at least for Scott. For the rest of us who loved him, it had just begun.

We all went back to Scott's parents' house for the repast. I simply could not believe I was in his childhood backyard with his family and so many of his childhood friends, without him. I imagined him as a little boy, playing in the grass. At every turn, with every person I spoke to, I missed him. I felt ill and couldn't eat. As one of the last to leave, I saw many sandwiches still left. Then I remembered Scott's words to me in the hospital: "What are we going to do with all the extra sandwiches?"

Ten days after Scott died, I had my first dream about him: I was driving to Boston to visit Scott, instead of my friend Jennifer. When I woke up, the dream felt real. Then I relived Scott's death, as I did every morning. Other times, the phone would ring, and I'd think it was him. Or something would happen during my day and, for a split second, I thought I could call him to share the news. My mind seemed to be playing evil little tricks on my heart.

I also had to deal with canceling the wedding plans. The dress shop had left a message saying all the dresses were in the store and ready for alterations. I called them back at lunchtime from my classroom at the hospital where I worked to let them know my fiancé had died. "There won't be any wedding," I said.

"You can't have a refund on the deposit for your dress, but you don't have to pay the balance," the woman from the store told me. "We can use it as a sample in the store." The thought of other brides trying on what was supposed to be my gown made me sick to my stomach. But that wasn't all. "The bridesmaids' dresses do have to be paid for."

"What?" I asked, beside myself as I thought of my six bridesmaids each paying two hundred twenty dollars.

"I'm sorry," the woman said. "But that's nonnegotiable."

"Even if the groom is dead?" I shrieked into the receiver.

"I'm sorry, but yes," she said. I felt terrible my friends had to pay for dresses they did not want and would not ever wear. I wished I had money to pay for all of them, but I didn't. I had cut my work schedule in half to be with Scott every day. Plus, we no longer had his income during the seven months he was sick. So I paid all our joint bills and all his credit card bills because I didn't want him to have bad credit. I had dreamed of us buying a house one day. I also had thought paying his credit card bills would somehow keep him alive.

My sister and all my friends paid that damn dress bill. Except Kristen. She was a student and broke like me. But she really did not want to pay because of the principle of the matter. So she didn't. The dress shop took her to small claims court. Kristen lost. Didn't these people have better things to do with their time? I was shocked by their lack of compassion. How many fiancés die? I'm sure it would not have hurt their business to take our wedding as a loss.

Other places made up for the callousness of the dress shop, though. The florist, photographer, and DJ refunded our deposits and sent heartfelt sympathy cards. They renewed my faith in people, and I decided to focus on their kindness.

Soon the time came for me to leave my second-floor apartment in the beautiful old Victorian. I couldn't bear to be there without Scott, but I also had a difficult time leaving. So I held one last party to help me leave on a happier note. On this last night, I didn't want to be alone. I wanted loving people around me.

I invited some of my friends who had come to know and love Scott. Most of the people who came were Scott's friends—people he had known since kindergarten growing up in Chatham and people he knew through his young adult life. Many of them I only knew through Scott; it felt just wrong for him not to be there. The apartment was completely empty, except for beer and snacks. We drank the beer directly from the bottles and ate the snacks right out of the bag. I had nothing left there. Absolutely nothing. I tried hard all night not to compare the apartment's current barren condition with its former full and lively state.

As I had no furniture, we all sat in a circle on the floor in the living room. Because the place was completely empty with no rugs, everything echoed as the sound vibrations bounced loudly off the hardwood floors and high ceilings. I looked around the room at all the people present to help make my departure less painful and felt an overwhelming sense of comfort. Scott had brought these people into my life, and because of him, they came to commemorate my departure from this loving home. I began to cry, partly because I missed Scott so much (missing him was always present for me), but also because I felt very loved.

Fortunately, Scott's best friend Chris always knew how to lighten a moment. He saw me crying, came over to me, and said, "I have an idea.

Let's play some Allman Brothers." Walking over to the portable CD player that someone brought, Chris popped in the Allman Brother's song, "Back to Where it All Begins." Taking my hands into his, he began dancing with me. Soon, everyone was off the floor and dancing. Scott would have loved us celebrating his life, celebrating our love for him, and celebrating how he had brought all of us together.

When the song finished, I looked at my watch. Although I had dreaded this moment, it was late—time to leave. I went over and turned the music off.

"Thank you everyone for coming." My words echoed throughout the room. "It means the world to me that you are all here."

"Group hug!" shouted Linda. We all headed for the center of the room and hugged each other.

As everyone gathered up their belongings, I headed toward the door to the stairway to see everyone out. It felt like the wedding receiving line that Scott and I never had. And there I stood alone, without him. Each person hugged me as they left; I could feel the love and concern in each embrace.

After everyone left, I took a few moments by myself. I stood where our bed had been, crying while remembering our tender lovemaking. I went to the window where he used to stand naked and call to me in the parking lot. I went into the bathroom and remembered the awful sight of dark blood streaking down his legs after the bone marrow extraction. I stood on the spot where he got down on one knee and proposed. I had to take it all in one last time and etch these sights and emotions in my memory.

When I walked out the door for the last time that night, I was grateful that I had been surrounded by good friends.

By some cruel twist of fate, all my closest friends left the area in the months just before and after Scott's death. They were moving on—for graduate school, jobs, relationships—and I was moving in with my parents, stuck in my grief.

One Saturday, a month after The Day After, I did nothing all day. I didn't even take a shower. I felt sick and depressed. Dad came in to my room. As he sat down on my bed next to me, I started to cry.

"Dad, this is my first time dealing with someone close to me dying," I said. "I can't make sense of it." My father, a man who usually had no lack of comforting words, did not seem to know what to say. He just hugged me. He listened. "Dad, I'm just so sad. So, so sad. I can't imagine that I am ever going to feel better. And I'm sad that Scott had to suffer. I'm sad that he was in so much pain. I'm sad that his last word to me was, 'Sorry.'" I'd not been able to share those thoughts and feelings with Scott while he was alive, leaving me with many unanswered questions. So I poured everything out to my dad.

"I don't know if Scott was afraid," I went on. "I don't know if he ever really knew that he was going to die. I don't know how he wants me to go on living without him."

For a time we sat in silence.

"I'm grateful that I was able to be there when he took his last breath," my father said as he cried. "He meant so much to me. It was a privilege to have been there. And not just me. I'm grateful that we all were there:

his parents, Chris, Mom. I just know he felt all of us holding him, loving him."

"I know. That's one thing that I do find comforting. I was there, holding his hand. I know he felt my love." I looked out my bedroom window toward the pool, remembering when my dad and Scott met there for the first time. We fell quiet. I imagined we were both thinking about Scott's final breath. Then Dad perked up.

"You know, if I have it my way," he said, "I'm going to die on a chairlift."

"Wouldn't you want to die while actually skiing?" I asked.

"Oh, no," he said. "I want to die on a chairlift, breathing in the cool mountain air. That's where I feel closest to God." We sat and hugged for another minute or two on the bed in my childhood bedroom, and I felt the comfort of years of love and care in this house. It was good to be home.

The next weekend, I walked with my dear friend Megan on both Saturday and Sunday mornings. Megan and I had been friends in elementary school and high school. At a time when it was uncommon to be friends with someone in a different grade, she and I were close. But we lost touch after high school. She sent me a sympathy card after Scott died, and she wrote her phone number in tiny numbers at the bottom corner of the page. I had great difficulty reading the numbers because she wrote them so small, trying to fit them on the page. I was glad she gave me her phone number. Many years later, I was unaware that she was back in town, and I no longer had her contact information. I decided to give her a call. She suggested that we walk. I welcomed the invitation.

Our walks became a regular healing practice for me. At a time when all my close friends had moved away, Megan moved back into town. Not only was I grateful to have a familiar face, but Megan had, and still has, an extraordinary gift of providing emotional comfort during times of grief and difficulty. She never tired of hearing my story. She tolerated my profound grief. She encouraged me to talk while we walked, and those walks brought me tremendous comfort.

One walk in particular remains clear in my mind. Megan and I were walking up Rolling Hill Road in Bernardsville. There's a steep section of the road where I found it difficult to walk and talk at the same time. But I continued talking, and gasping, because what I had to say could not wait.

"Megan, I cannot bear another loss. Ever. Losing Scott now has me worried about losing anyone else. I could not bear it. I am afraid of my father dying. I don't know how I could bear losing my father."

Megan normalized my feelings, explaining that it's not unusual to experience heightened fears of loss after a loved one has passed away. As always, she made me feel understood, less crazy, and less alone.

I came home, showered, and was reading one of the various books I had purchased to help me process my loss and grief. Sitting on my bed and looking around my childhood bedroom at all of the pink, I recalled my excitement when the pink carpet was installed ten years ago. My mother and I had painted the pink walls together. Lost in my thoughts, I remembered my sixteen-year-old self when my father interrupted my memories by knocking on my door. He had just returned from his run. "You know Mr. Heinrich around the corner?" Dad asked. "The old man in the little white house near the road? He was asking about you. He asked if you were the young lady whose fiancé died." I'd passed that house hundreds of times on my running route. Mr. Heinrich was often doing yard work as I ran by. "I guess he read about in the paper." Leaning over, I cupped my face in my hands, and I cried and cried. Dad held me. I cried at the thought of the tenderness of this sweet old man around the corner who felt concerned about me. I imagined that he knew my pain. He was always alone outside. I thought that his wife must have died many years ago.

"I'm sorry for making you cry," Dad said.

"You're not making me cry, Dad. I'm sad all the time."

"I'm having a tough time, too," Dad said, "but what helps me is knowing that Scott would not want me to be sad. He would want me to keep smiling, so that is what I try to do. I know he would not want me to be unhappy. I know he would not want you to be sad, either."

"I can't imagine a time when I will ever *not* be grief-stricken, and that scares me, too."

"I assure you, dear, you will not feel this way forever," he said. "You will be happy again."

"Promise me, Dad. Promise me that I will be happy again because I can't bear this."

"I promise you," he said with conviction. I added another fear.

"Dad, I'm afraid that I will never find someone to love again. Or ever be loved like Scott has loved me." Dad hugged me even more tightly, and I cried even harder.

"You are special, Peg," my dad said. "When the time is right, you will love again, and you will be loved again. I have no doubt about that." I had to believe him.

Later that day, my dad did his usual hooting and howling at a football game on television. When a friend called, he learned Okemo Mountain

Resort, one of his favorite ski areas in Vermont, was open. Spontaneously, Dad decided to go skiing. Excited, he walked around in his ski outfit for hours, showing me the duct tape on his pants, strategically placed so snow wouldn't get in the hole. He put on his heavy ski boots, saying he was "breaking them in" for the next day.

"It's taking you a long time to pack, Dad," I said.

"I have a lot to get ready," he replied. "Okemo has three slopes open, and I'm going to ski for three days!" He prepared his breakfast for the morning—a bagel with jelly—and, as usual, he left jelly on the kitchen cabinets, the refrigerator handle, and the staircase banister.

Dad said he was going to bed early since he'd be leaving in the middle of the night for Vermont. Later, I heard him get up and walk to the first floor. He told Mom he came downstairs for a second good night kiss because he was having trouble sleeping. Before departing at 3:00 a.m., he wrote a note saying he'd see us Wednesday and left it on the kitchen counter. I smiled when I read the sweet love note for my mother.

I worked half a day and then went to the mall to Christmas shop, trying to get back to a regular routine. When I returned home, I got on the treadmill and mindlessly exercised. The treadmill was in a room at the top of the second staircase that used to be my sister's room, tucked away in a corner of the house. Her room had become our exercise room with a rowing machine, stationery recumbent bicycle, treadmill, and free weights. The room was located over the garage and didn't have proper insulation. It always felt hot in the summer and cold in the winter. My mom entered the cold room with a terrible look on her face.

"Peg, I have to talk to you," she said. "It's Dad." I looked at her but kept walking on the treadmill. I didn't want to hear what she had to say.

I thought if I stayed on the treadmill, the loud humming sound would drown out whatever horrible news she had to share with me. Since I didn't stop, she had to ask me.

"Would you please get off the treadmill?"

Like a petulant child, I complied. My mother walked toward me and put her hands on my shoulders. "He had a heart attack on the mountain," she said. *Was he dead?* I thought, but I knew he was by looking at her face.

"No!" I screamed. "No! Oh, my God. Not Dad." There we stood, holding each other—two young widows.

After a time, I walked downstairs to find a police officer in my kitchen. While I had been upstairs, he had entered to give my mother the news. I hadn't heard him over the treadmill.

Finally, my mother and I stopped crying enough to start making those dreaded phone calls. Again. This was not right. Scott's parents came over and sat with us for hours. Scott's best friends, Chris and Doug, came over, too.

I went to bed that night questioning my existence. With Scott's passing, I lost my future. With my father's passing, I lost part of my past and who I was. *How was I going to make sense of my life and keep them both alive inside me?*

The next day, we learned more about my father's death from members of the Okemo Mountain Ski Patrol who drove his Bronco from Vermont back to our house in New Jersey. The man and woman told us my father was already dead by the time his chair reached the dismount hill. The poor, young lift attendant did not know what to do.

They gave us my father's ski clothes. I was shocked to see blood on them. They apologized that the ski jacket was ripped, stating that they'd had to cut off his clothing to get to his chest. But why blood? I didn't want to know.

My mother prepared dinner and invited them to stay.

"The entire Okemo family was affected," the woman said during the meal. "It was a sad, sad day for the mountain."

I wanted details about my father's death, and I wondered if these two could provide me some information. *When did he die? Had anyone seen him skiing?* I hoped that this was not his only chair lift ride—that he had enjoyed at least one run.

I knew that if I asked what time he died, I would know my answer. My father always liked to be at the mountain early, ready to get on the lift as soon as it opened. Oh how he loved to get "first chair." I mustered the courage to ask.

"What time did he die?" I could feel my lips quivering. "Do you know about what time he got to the top of the chairlift?"

Without hesitation and with certainty, the man provided a time that I wanted to hear. "10:30," he said softly. Never had a time meant so much to me. *He skied! He skied!*

As if he sensed why I was asking, he added, "People saw him skiing. He was hard to miss!" I knew exactly what he meant. Not only was my father wearing a bright red jacket, but he had an unforgettable way of skiing–with his arms outstretched, casually making wide turns, listening to his tunes. His skiing style exuded happiness. Dad was easy to spot.

This kind man, who had driven my father's Bronco all the way down to New Jersey from Vermont, reached over and put his hand on my forearm, gently squeezed it and said, "He skied." Then he did the same to my mother, repeating softly, "He skied."

I was overcome with emotion. I recalled my father's words. "You know, if I have it my way, I'm going to die on a chairlift, breathing in the cool mountain air. That's where I feel closest to God." I was so grateful to know with certainty that my father was able to experience what brought him great comfort and peace, and that he was able to die exactly how he wished, when his time came. *But his time came way too soon.*

My father died three days before Thanksgiving. He had just turned fifty-eight: his birthday had been just eight days after Scott died. Relatives spent Thanksgiving with us and high school friends home for the holiday visited. Many people stopped by with food or stayed to provide company, but no one wanted to sit in Dad's chair. I envisioned my dad sitting there with corn on the cob stuck in his teeth or his shirt pulled over his head to make us laugh. At the end of the evening, I drove Aunt Ruth home, all by myself, taking over the duty for Scott and my father.

Two of my friends, Nancy and Jennifer, came over much later when they arrived in town. We sat around my childhood kitchen table. I wanted to be a child again, etching my initials on the side of the table, eating a meal my mother had made after my dad came home from work.

Being with these two friends comforted me. I had known Nancy since fifth grade, and Jennifer since seventh grade. Rather than talking about death and dying, we reminisced about great memories from high school and early adulthood. I welcomed the light-hearted conversation, and I felt close to these two women who had seen me through so much—and still were.

"Remember when you dragged us to Vermont after college?" Jennifer asked.

"What do you mean, 'dragged you,' Jennifer? You loved it!"

"It smelled like cow poop everywhere! It was SO stinky!" she laughed.

"Yes! Remember we stepped out of our hotel and all lifted our shirt collars to cover our noses? It was so stinky!" Nancy chimed in.

"Well, that's because we were right next to a farm. Vermont does have farms you know! And I hope you remember more than the stinkiness! How about our beautiful drive over Smugggler's Notch? How about the cute boys that tried to pick us up at Rasputin's?" I asked.

"And that place was stinky too! And the floor was so sticky!" Jennifer recalled.

"We're just joshin', Peg. We loved that trip!" Nancy said. "Even though it WAS stinky!"

We laughed some more as we reminisced about funny times from junior high and high school. It felt good to recall these special times. I felt grateful that we had been an integral part of each other's lives for so many years.

As night fell, we turned on the outside light, which shone on the deck where Scott and I had had our engagement party three months earlier. In the light, we saw a gentle snow fall straight down in large flakes—the kind of snow that has always made me feel peaceful.

The next day, another wake. When we arrived at the funeral home, I was nervous to look at my sweet father in the casket. Since he'd had a heart attack, I was afraid he'd have a look of fear or pain on his face. Mom, Debbie, Brian, David, and I approached Dad with our arms around each other, all in a line.

"He's smiling!" said David, speaking first. "Dad is smiling!" He was right. Dad's eyes were even smiling. I felt relieved. I had an image of him seeing "the light," or Scott, or God at his moment of death. Just like he said, he must have been at peace on the chairlift, breathing in the cool mountain air.

Between sessions of the wake, we all came back to our house where we ate dinner in the dining room. I couldn't finish my meal and went up to my room to lie down.

The day of my father's funeral was sunny, just like Scott's. When we arrived by limousine and entered the church, everyone had already arrived. Again, the church was full. On this day, I also found it difficult to walk by college friends, work friends, high school friends, and grade school friends on my way down the aisle.

Despite my profound sorrow, I was able to share thoughts about my dad in a eulogy:

> I do feel one of the richest people alive, from all the love my father gave to his family. He was a real family man. He lived for his wife and children. I had the best childhood. My mom and dad took us to every park, campground, zoo, and attraction in the area. We had a trailer in the Poconos where we would spend our summer weekends as a family.
>
> This was a man who in his free time chose to take his four children and five of their friends to the trailer for a fun-filled weekend. I can just see him now, driving the station wagon with nine grammar school children laughing and screaming. He planned out the whole weekend with games and events that he called our own little Olympics, complete with awards and prizes. He was in his glory.

As the family grew older, we continued to spend our free time together. After David graduated from college in Colorado, the family rented a van and toured the Southwest together. Dad would often drive up to Vermont to ski with me for the weekend while I was in school. We had many ski trips out west together. . . .

Being alone with his wife also meant so much to him. In his journal, he wrote:

"Carol and I got drenched in Jockey Hollow Park. I looked at her walking ahead of me and it felt so good. Feeling close to her and how special it is when we do something together."

I will never forget the happiness and warmth I felt as I watched my parents dance the first dance at Debbie's wedding last year. He was hugging Mom so tight and crying. It was one of the happiest days of his life to see his daughter so happy with a wonderful man. . . .

My dad made friends wherever he went. He talked to strangers and found comfort in being with his fellow human beings. He often spoke of other people's good nature and how seeing that in other people made him feel good. He said he was touched by all the support from his colleagues at work after the death of my fiancé. He also spoke so highly of his best friend, Ron Shiner, who he thought was a saint, and the rest of his ski buddies in the Poconos. They all meant so much to him. . . .

In closing, I would like to read a Father's Day card that I gave to Dad two years ago. Since he saved it, I know it meant a lot to him, and I would like him to hear it once more.

Dear Dad,

Thank you for being the wonderful person that you are. You have taught me so much about life, and I am forever grateful. You have served as a great role model with an inspiring outlook on life. Not only are you a wonderful father, but you are a wonderful person. You are nice to everyone who crosses your path, and you greet everyone with a smile. You are able to laugh at yourself. You have so many qualities that deserve admiration and respect. You are a pleasant person to be around with your combination of goofiness and good humor. You make others happy, and that is an incredible gift. I also consider myself lucky to have a father with whom I can share so much. Our walks, talks, bike rides, and ski trips mean so much. The times that I am able to share with you are precious. I love you so much, Dad, for all you do, for the person you are, and for having such an important role in my life.

Love, Peggy.

Dad, you will live in my heart forever.

# Ring of Power

November 28, 1994

The Monday after my father's funeral, I went back to work. I did not want to take any more time off. I needed to keep things normal and stay busy. I worked at a hospital-based preschool in Newark with young children exposed to crime, poverty, domestic violence, shootings, prostitution, and drug deals. I found peace in my work. It was like these four-year-old children knew pain when they saw it. I did not say a word to them about my losses. They had seen more tragedy in their short lives than most people do in a lifetime. Maybe they could see the sadness in my eyes, though. I don't know, but I believe they had no idea how much they were doing for me every day with their hugs and kisses. Every "I love you, Miss Peggy" was balm for my broken heart.

But being at home felt different. Home was a reminder of how much I'd lost. I was in my childhood home without my father, bearing witness to my mother's grief. I hurt for her intensely because I, too, had lost my partner. I never imagined my mother and I would be widows at the same time in our lives.

For a while, my mother did not know what her financial situation would be. My father was the traditional breadwinner, and he'd always given us a comfortable life. My mother didn't know how much life insurance he had or how it would help with daily and yearly living expenses. For a time, she was afraid to spend any money at all, which meant running the dishwasher or other household machines infrequently and keeping the lights off. The house was dark. We were living in an emotional and physical tomb.

I needed to talk about my father and Scott all the time. I appreciated everyone who would listen and tolerate my grief. I appreciated those who were not afraid to say their names, those who shared their own stories of loss, and those who communicated their support through their behavior or the unspoken understanding in their eyes.

Two occasions were particularly special. Scott's family invited me to dinner for his birthday. On my way to their house, a song came on the radio that made me believe Scott was with me—Lenny Kravitz's "Are You Gonna Go My Way." Scott loved dancing to that tune. Every time I heard it, I smiled, thinking about Scott taking off his robe and wiggling his butt at me.

During the dinner with Scott's family, we each shared a story about a song being played at a certain time, undeniably reminding us that Scott is still with us.

"It's only natural that Scott communicates through songs," his mother remarked. "Music is all he cared about." Then his sister Jill chimed in.

"And Peggy," she said, squeezing my hand.

The second occasion of special support occurred while I was in Breckenridge, Colorado, with my ski friends. These friends did not know Scott well, and another couple, Mary Rose and Jason, had never even met him. I was with this group of friends in Colorado on March 18, 1995, our ill-fated wedding day. I was touched when Mary Rose got everyone in a circle and asked that we all hold hands and think about him.

Some days, I thought I was going crazy. Other days, I felt the weight of carrying two proverbial tons of sorrow, one on each of my shoulders. I often felt physically ill and cried myself to sleep, thinking my mother was doing the same down the hall. Other days, I struggled to get out of bed. I always did, though, because I worried that if I didn't, I would only fall deeper into the black pit of grief. I wrote in my diary:

> I will never have another father. I feel like my childhood is really gone. And my future died with Scott. Who knows what will even happen to me? I can't imagine being lucky enough to love and be loved like it was with Scott. I don't want anyone else. I just want them back.

I was afraid of losing them even more by getting used to their not being around, and I wondered if I was making Scott's death the center of my life so that I might miss the opportunity of something new. I even spoke to my hair colorist about my losses. The last time I had seen him was the day before my engagement party, when Scott felt great and everything seemed to be looking brighter. Although I had been going to this hairdresser for five years, I never felt that I connected with him. He always appeared distant and aloof. But when your hair colorist asks how you're doing, and something huge is going on, it's hard not to mention it. So I told him that Scott died.

"Don't dwell on it," he said. I wondered what I must have sounded like to get an unhelpful response like that. Then he offered me a free coloring, calling the service a "bereavement gift." He meant to be kind, but he pissed me off. For heaven's sake, it had only been six months since the love of my life died. I never went back.

I tried to go out as often as I could. I was twenty-six years old. That's what single, twenty-six-year-olds do. They go out. I was grateful to have people to go out with, but at times I felt guilty enjoying myself, even for a minute, because my fiancé had just suffered so much and died.

The first time I really laughed was while I was visiting Nancy on New York City's Upper West Side. Nancy's boyfriend, Scott, met us in her tiny studio apartment. Then the three of us met two of our friends from high school, Jamie and Tom. In high school, they'd been two of my closest "guy friends" though we'd lost touch after college. Jamie and Tom felt bad about everything I had been through that year. They wanted to spend some time with me. I was comforted by that gesture alone. The five of us went out to dinner and then picked a different venue for drinks. Before parting ways, we stood on a street corner, not wanting the night to end. We reminisced about our great days at Bernards High School.

"Remember the Smoking Lounge?" I asked. "I can't believe we used to have a designated spot for students to smoke outside!"

"And the gross wrestling mats in the gym!" Nancy recalled. "Those mats were sticky, and the room smelled horrible."

"Speaking of smelly, who was it that always set off stink bombs in the hallways?" Tom asked.

"I don't know who was responsible for that!" Jamie responded. "But I do remember Dave Armstrong giving us all marbles to pass along to Dr. McCain as he shook our hands at graduation. The poor guy didn't know what to do with all those marbles!"

"Remember that time you farted in Biology?" Tom blurted out. We all laughed so hard. I nearly peed in my pants. I completely forgot my grief, but when the moment passed, it returned along with a dose of guilt.

I then heard my father's voice speaking to me, reminding me of what had helped him: "Scott would not want me to be sad." He was right. I also knew my dad wouldn't want me to be grieving. I wondered if my tears made them cry in heaven. Grief is such an emotionally topsy-turvy state. I allowed myself to experience this craziness and despair for a while and then embraced the notion that my happiness would not betray them. Yet I also told myself I had so much baggage that no man in his right mind would date me. I convinced myself there was no one in the world strong enough to be with me.

During this time I realized my engagement ring had become a symbol of where I was in my process of letting go and moving on. I wore it on different fingers, depending on how I felt, which sometimes changed within a day. On days I wanted to feel close to Scott, had no interest in moving on, or felt terrified for the future, I put it on the ring finger of my left hand, exactly where he had placed it.

On March 27, 1995, I wrote in my diary: "We are supposed to be on our honeymoon right now. I put my engagement ring back on my finger. What for?"

A remarkable thing happened one day at my job at the preschool. One of the five-year-old girls with whom I shared a connection was gazing at my ring. She held my hand, pulled it closer to her eyes, ran her fingers over it.

"Your ring is so powerful," she said. To her, it was a piece of jewelry, but she sensed its significance.

The power of the ring held me, too.

I surprised myself when my dear friend Megan offered to do a Reiki session with me. I learned in my quest for anything spiritual that Reiki is a healing technique involving a laying on of hands for the purpose of channeling energy and restoring physical and emotional well-being.

"Peggy," Megan said. "I know you're in so much emotional pain right now. I would love to offer you a Reiki session. I believe it can help you with your pain, help you to heal."

Rather than comfort me, which was her pure intention, the very thought of a session scared me to death. Immediately, I turned her down.

"Oh, Megan, that is sweet of you, but I'm terrified." At that point, I interpreted any kind of healing as letting go, and I was not ready to let go. "I know it sounds crazy, but right now I'm terrified of healing. I feel as though with every step toward my healing, I'm losing my connection to Scott. My pain and grief are my connection to him," I said sadly. I added as I cried, "They're all I have left."

In her ever so comforting voice, she said, "I understand." She didn't even need to say it. I knew she understood.

Some days, I put the ring on the ring finger of my right hand. To me, that was progress. I was not telling the world: "I'm taken." But wearing the ring on my right hand still kept me close to Scott. Only rarely did I keep the ring in my jewelry box.

This great ambivalence shifted when I visited a wise woman named Shirley, who was married to my father's best friend, Ron. Shirley had known me since I was ten years old. We'd been together every weekend while skiing at Big Boulder. Ron and my father went to New Zealand together to celebrate turning fifty. She showed me a book about the spiritual meanings behind certain creatures, including bald eagles.

"Take it home," she said. "Read it." She explained that in Native American culture, seeing a bald eagle was considered a sign that the spirit of a loved one was near. Oh, how I could not wait to see a bald eagle! I had never seen one before. Shirley also encouraged me to keep my engagement ring on my right hand.

"You'll never meet a man if you keep it on your left hand, at least not the kind of man you want to meet," she said. "Peggy, people who have had a great love, like you did with Scott, are very capable of loving again. There will be a next time for you, and it will be very special. You will feel so alive."

I believed her. Just seeing Shirley with Ron gave me hope since their marriage was the second one for both of them. Her first husband died suddenly after being struck by a bus. She was living proof that finding love again was possible. I took her advice: the ring never returned to my left hand, but I couldn't take it off completely.

Having the ring on my right hand didn't summon Prince Charming into my life because I wasn't emotionally ready for him. I didn't want to be alone, but it was just too soon. So God, or the Universe, sent me a series of men who were safe, meaning they were all wrong for me.

I met the first one, Bob, at a bereavement group. He was kind, and we bonded because we'd both lost our partners. He showed me pictures of his beautiful wife, who met her untimely death at the age of thirty-three from a terminal illness. We shared coffee after the bereavement group and stories over dinner. I wanted to feel something for him because he was nice. But the timing was wrong. I simply felt too lost in my grief, just as he was in his. But he provided me with company and empathy and made me feel attractive when my grief made me feel ugly. I hoped I did the same for him.

As we drove to Bob's friend's house for our first date, "Sister Golden Hair" came on the radio. When we got there, "Blue Sky" by the Allman

Brothers was playing. I couldn't help thinking of Scott when our songs were playing. I envisioned him singing the words of the song to me. *What is going on?* Things got even more strange when one of Bob's friends introduced me to another one of his friends as "Peggy Unger."

When Scott was alive, I had never uttered the words "Peggy Unger." I never even thought that name. That last name was for later, after we were married. I'd hoped that if I never said the name, he just had to live to our wedding. After he died, I never expected to hear it. So when this person said "Peggy Unger," it took my breath away. I wanted to cry, but I couldn't. I was sitting in a room full of people that I didn't know in a stranger's house. I saw that Bob perceived my pain, and it meant a lot to me that he understood.

Bob sent me flowers for Valentine's Day. I know he meant well, but they made me sad. I wanted them to be from Scott, who'd been dead for four months. I was not ready to receive flowers from another man. I also intuited that Bob wanted to be giving those lovely flowers to his deceased wife. Actually, the flowers made me sad for both of us. A week later, I told him I did not want a relationship, which was a difficult thing to do because I knew what he was going through. I didn't want to hurt him more. My grief caused me to be a little selfish and focus on my own needs.

Months later, my next date with a different man turned into a nightmare and should probably be in *Guinness World Records* for the worst date ever. I drove myself to Peter's house in Pennsylvania. He lived close to our dinner destination. I should have had a clue about what I was in for when he told me he wanted to get himself some groceries before he took me to dinner. At the grocery store, he suggested that I should buy him cereal and bananas instead of him buying me flowers. *OK. Weird.* Then we dropped off his groceries at his house where there was a keg attached to his refrigerator. He said he liked to keep large amounts of cold beer available at all times.

Finally, Peter took me to a steak and lobster fundraiser at a first aid squad. I don't like steak or lobster. Whatever. So much for asking your date what she would like to do. He proceeded to get drunk quickly, picked a fight with an Emergency Medical Technician (EMT) on the squad, and got thrown out of the party.

As we walked to the parking lot, I told him, "I am NOT getting in the car with you. You're drunk. And I don't want to drive your car."

He slurred his words, "Whatta we gonna do?" He paused, "Lemme call Joe. He lives nearby." So he called his friend to pick us up. Thankfully, his friend came quickly. But he didn't come fast enough!

While stumbling, Peter said, "I gotta pee!" Before I could turn away, he unzipped his pants. Losing his balance, he took a step back and bumped into his car. Then he pulled down his pants and urinated in the parking lot, right in front of me. I looked at the puddle that his urine created on the asphalt. I couldn't believe my eyes. *Holy crap! Is this what I'm in for with this dating business?* The stark contrast to how polite and respectful Scott was made me want to cry. If I weren't so shocked, I would have cried.

The next man I dated was nice like Bob, but also, like Bob, quite wrong for me. I felt attracted to Paul because he was smart, played the piano beautifully, cooked well, and was interested in all sorts of spiritual things that intrigued me at the time. But even though I was in search of the meaning of life and all things spiritual, he was too woo-woo for me.

One day he asked me to help him post announcements around his neighborhood inviting his neighbors to a party.

"How nice," I said. "What's the party for?"

"To celebrate the trees," he replied. *OK, I'm out.*

My next dates were with someone who was even more wrong for me. I broke up with him after learning, over time, that he liked to smoke lots of pot. Everyone is free to do what they want, but drugs were just not my thing. Additionally, he didn't have a job or a place to live and, oh, there was one other little problem. He was arrested for having a concealed handgun. *Lovely. Bye-bye. What was I thinking?*

All these men were easy to date because I knew in my heart the relationships were going nowhere, fast. They weren't horrible people. In fact, they were all quite kind. Even peeing Peter was nice, when he wasn't drinking. But, despite their moments of thoughtfulness, they were all wrong for me.

# Return of Passion

## November, 1994

Because I was just twenty-six and without my life partner, I felt lonely. Grief is a solitary experience, but somehow, I felt even more alone with peers. Young adults my age could not empathize with what I was going through. They were getting married and having children. How could they possibly understand? My dearest friends tried, and they were there for me whenever I needed them, but I also sensed that I scared them. So I often held back. The bereavement group provided me with an outlet where I didn't need to hold back or worry about scaring anyone with my profound grief or thoughts of death.

Since the group was helpful to me, I thought it might help my mother, too. I brought her with me just one week after my father died. Maybe it was too soon. After I parked and got out of the driver's side, I expected her to get out, too. But she didn't. I went over to her side of the car and opened the door.

"What's the matter, Mom?"

"I can't go in. I don't belong here."

"I know, Mom. Neither of us belongs here. But this group has been helpful for me. I can't leave you in the car. Come inside. Everyone is really nice." I tried everything to get her out of the car. "I wouldn't have brought you if I didn't think it would be helpful." I leaned in the car toward her and put my hand on her elbow, gently tugging at her.

"C'mon, Mom. I mean it. This will be helpful." I sensed her sorrow. I remembered how I felt when I walked in my first time. I was crying so hard, my tears wet the sign-in sheet. I knew exactly how she was feeling. Tears streamed down my face. It was just so wrong that both of us were there for a bereavement group! I wanted to scream, "We don't belong here!" I felt a pit in my stomach as I thought that it was only one year ago that Scott had asked my father for his blessing in asking me to marry him. Now they both were dead. I tried to put these thoughts aside. My goal was to get my mother out of the car. Finally, she gave in, and we walked slowly toward the door, our arms wrapped around each other's shoulders.

By that time, the meeting had already begun. We quietly entered and took our seats next to each other. Maybe it was just me, but I noticed that the men her age and older were looking at her. Why wouldn't they? She was stunning. She was young. She was only fifty-two and, clearly, she was now single. I was very uncomfortable seeing other men look at my mother.

After the second session, two of the men asked my mother out on a date. That was not what I had intended! At first, she refused, but one in particular persisted. She and Ed went to dinner for their first dates, and then she brought him to our house for dinner. Ed was also a widow, and he had been attending the bereavement group after his wife Mary passed away. I was happy for my mother, but it was at first difficult for me to see her with someone else. I had only known her with my father, and my father had died just three months earlier. It was all so much for me to take in.

One night while the two of us were eating dinner, I said, "Mom, I'm happy that you're spending time with someone, and it's fine that you bring him to the house. But PLEASE don't hold hands in front of me," I demanded. I was surprised at my own demand. And I continued. "Please don't show any kind of affection in front of me. And I absolutely do not want to see him sitting in Dad's chair."

My mother didn't ask why, because she already knew. Seeing her moving on with Ed reminded me of what I had lost. Warmly, she responded, "OK, dear." My mother has always intuitively known how to respond to my emotional needs without my explaining anything, and I always loved her for that. Especially then.

I had to admire her courage. I was grateful that Ed made her happy and for the bravery she modeled for me. She was allowing her heart to love again. Some may have thought her new relationship came too soon after my father's death, but there are people on this earth who are so filled with love that they must share it with someone. My mother is one of them.

Soon we learned that Scott and Ed's wife Mary had died on the same day and that our two families had shared the funeral home. They were the ones I worried about bothering because Scott's wake was as loud as a frat party.

All during this time, weird happenings provided me with the comfort that my loved ones were with me and that there is much more to the world that we don't understand.

I'm glad my mother was with me for one of these happenings, or it simply would not be believable. Before I began the demands of my doctoral program, the two of us decided to go to California and visit my brother David in Tahoe. We planned to drive a portion of the Pacific Coast Highway that would have been included in my honeymoon trip with Scott. I was comforted to be doing this trip with my mother. She was a brave woman—quiet but strong. I was happy she agreed to accompany me on the trip.

We sat at a traffic light at Half Moon Bay, just south of San Francisco, waiting to turn left onto the highway. Since the radio reception was filled with static, I fiddled with the stations as we waited. To my sheer joy, on came our wedding song, "I Can See Clearly Now." As I drove, I looked over at my mother in the passenger seat. She quickly turned to look at me with her mouth wide open. She placed her hand on my shoulder.

"He's here," she said. "This is your wedding song. This is your honeymoon. Of course, he's here!" We both burst into tears.

In trying to make sense of my grief and the spirit world, I visited mediums. I was struggling with the meaning in their deaths, life beyond death, the meaning of life, but most of all, the meaning of the rest of my life. Two mediums were recommended to me.

For one, I had to travel to New York City. Even though I grew up just ninety minutes west of what many consider the greatest city in the world, I never visited New York as a child with my family. Instead, we went to the mountains. So I felt a bit of trepidation, mixed with childhood wonder, at the prospect of going into Manhattan. I wasn't happy that I had to travel by myself to see this elderly woman, but my friend told me she was worth every penny of the two hundred dollars she charged for a reading. She assured me I would not be disappointed.

After welcoming me to her brownstone in Greenwich Village, she held my hand and guided me to the room where she did her readings, just a few steps off the foyer. We sat across from each other at an oversized card table covered in a dark tablecloth. The table appeared way too large for the small space. The room was dark and dingy without windows. I felt like I was in a closet. A few crystals and rocks were displayed on a small table against the wall. Though pretty, they could have been showcased in a more eye-pleasing manner. A makeshift curtain hung in the doorway, serving as a barrier to the next room.

"Uncross your legs, my dear, and give me your hands," she said gently. She took my hands in hers and asked me to close my eyes. Instantly, I felt comforted. She began speaking very softly.

"What was the name that was given to you when you were born in this life?"

"Margaret Susan Doherty," I replied, my tone soft enough to match hers.

"Ah. Before we begin, there are a couple of things you should know. I am looking at vibration patterns. It is my job to look at the pattern and to translate them in some way so that they make sense to you. I want to make that clear so that you don't think that there is some big guy in the sky who is whispering in my ear." She paused. "Why have you come here today?"

"My fiancé and my father died last year," I replied, sadly. "I'd like to make some sort of contact with them. If possible."

"Ah. We'll see. Give me their names."

"My fiancé was Scott Unger, and my father, Bill Doherty."

"When did they die?"

"Scott died October 11$^{th}$ and my father November 21$^{st}$."

"Ah, a hard time for you. Alright. This is going to take a minute. Well, Scott looks to me as if he were very good natured. Hmm. Kind of a— you know, he could make you laugh and make you believe in the future and make you believe that everything was—if he was around, you know life was going to be alright. If he could be in his body now, he'd kind of say, 'Hey, it's going to be OK. Have a beer.'" She continued to describe him.

"He was a total optimist with this enormous amount of good will and energy always coming through from him, and it still does. Now because of this, I don't see him as being very sick. Either he wasn't sick, or it just never got him. I don't see the gloom and the upset that come along with people who are sick for a very long time. But he didn't want to be sick. He was big on the good times. The guys, the parties. The times with you he planned on. But he would rather have died than to live in any way impaired. He just wanted to make a wonderful life for you, for his family, and for the children to come. What did he die of? I see something in the head." I was reluctant to reveal anything, as I wanted to make sure she was the real deal and not just using what information I gave her. But I betrayed myself.

"He had cancer," I said.

"No, no," she said. "That's not why he died." I thought, *What are you talking about, lady? He had cancer. That is how he died. Am I wasting my money?* Then she said something that took my breath away.

"I keep hearing a *bzzz* sound, like an electrical circuit gone haywire, like a little red short circuit. Not a tumor. Like a *bzzz*, a kind of electrical disconnection in the brain." She paused. "Was he ever struck by lightning?" *Holy crap! Yes, he was!* The odds are about one in a million that anyone will be struck by lightning in any given year. How could she have known?

"The strike did something to his brain," she went on, "and his whole nervous system went haywire, allowing the cancer to grow." I continued to sit, legs uncrossed, eyes closed, as instructed. I didn't want to do anything that would interfere with the spirits "coming through." I didn't want to move a muscle, which meant I didn't let go of her hand to reach for the tissue I desperately needed. Blobs of mucus ran down from my nostrils, but I stayed still as a statue.

As if she could read my mind, she said, "I don't think he's so crazy about thinking about you getting married to someone else, although he's all for that," she said. *There's the answer to the question that I always wanted to ask Scott, but never could because Scott never wanted to talk about such things—Did he want me to move on and get married one day, and how would he feel about that?* I felt a connection to him, believing that he still thought of me as only his.

"What he does want for you is to have children. He thinks you're going to be a wonderful mother." I remembered all of our conversations about children. I knew he thought I was going to be a wonderful mother, but it was nice to hear it. And I always thought the same of him. My mind wandered to seeing him on that couch with his housemate's two children when I surprised him by coming home. I remembered him not flinching while catching the regurgitated food of the sweet three-year-old girl in my care in Colorado.

She continued. "He surely did love being loved by you, being loved so much. He just loved that you admired him. The only thing he wants to make sure you know is that he didn't give up." *I know he didn't give up! Why would he even say this? I know he fought with every ounce of his being. He wanted to live!*

"He wants to spend the year with you. He's still too real here. He's still too with you, and I don't see him ready to go until next Fall or at least a year after his death. He might be out of the body, but it's still a relationship. He wants to spend the year with you. He likes hanging around you." *Oh, Scott, I knew it! I just knew it! I can feel you around me. I feel your presence every day, my dear.* She shifted gears and spoke about my father.

"Now this looks like something sudden, like a heart attack or a stroke. He knew what it was. He thought that Scott's death was unjust, that it shouldn't have happened. He was such a good person, he loved you, he was young. But with the heart attack, your father did not feel that it was unjust. It's almost as if he's saying, 'Well, this I understand. This is OK. That one was not OK.' He felt complete in his life." I was comforted to hear that my father felt as though he had lived a full life. But I did not feel that way! *I still want you here, Dad!*

Even though I was fortunate to have had many experiences that assured me there was life after death and that I was still connected to Scott and my father, I was comforted by the added guidance and lovely voice of this elderly expert of the spirit world.

Three months later, someone suggested to me that I see another medium who'd already been recommended to me by someone else. I felt I was meant to go see her. Plus, she was only a thirty-minute drive from my house in New Jersey. She didn't charge any money for her service, I was told, because she considered her ability a gift freely given by God to be shared with others. I thought that philosophy meant she must be the real deal.

There was one catch, though: She booked three months in advance and, by the time of my appointment, she could be dead. *What? Dead?* She was, after all, old and sick. I was instructed to call the morning of my appointment to hear an outgoing message on an answering machine stating whether she was alive or dead and whether to come for the appointment or not.

I patiently waited three months and then called the number on the morning of my appointment. *She was alive!* I drove to her church in Wharton. After ringing the bell on the outside of the small house next to the church, I waited for what seemed a long time before she answered the door. Greeting me with a handshake with her right hand, she then covered the outside of my hand with her left. Letting go, she waved for me to follow her up the stairs. She walked very slowly and held the banister tightly.

The room at the top of the stairs looked like a small living room—cozy and inviting but with minimal furniture and decorations. We sat on two cushioned, upholstered chairs, facing each other. To my left was a small table.

When I made the appointment, I'd been instructed to bring a blank cassette tape to record the reading. The tape player was resting on the table next to us. I handed her the cassette tape and her fingers struggled with the machine as she tried to put in a cassette tape for me. She, too, told me to uncross my legs, and then we began.

"Who's Bill?" she asked. I gasped. She didn't mess around.

"My father," I said, immediately sobbing.

"It's very important to him that he make his presence known," she said. "So I had to say his name right away to make him be quiet!" I was ecstatic that my father came through, but I also wanted Scott to come through.

"Is there anyone else?" I asked. "My fiancé Scott died, and I was hoping to receive messages from him, too."

"How did he die?" she asked. I didn't want to give her too much information, but I already trusted her.

"He had cancer."

"You're blaming the cancer, but he's not." That was just what the other medium had said! "Who is John? You've got John around you."

"I do not know a John," I replied. "Oh, maybe his business partner?" He was the only John I could think of.

"No. Not that John," she said. "But you do, or you will, have a John around you. Your father wants your mother to marry again, and you will marry again." She paused. "But Scott cautions, 'When you meet someone, don't put me on a pedestal. No man will ever match up. Not even

I.' And you will have children. He's got little children lined up for you, and at least one will be a boy. Your father wants you to name your son after him. Not your son's first name, but his middle name." I let my mind wander to my future son with the middle name of William. The future to which she alluded seemed very far away from where I was emotionally. I still only wanted to be with Scott. She seemed to sense my thoughts.

"You will feel Scott around you until the second anniversary of his death," she said. "Then you will have room for another man in your life. But there will always be a part of your heart that belongs to him, and he likes that. He warns again: 'Just don't put me on a pedestal.' Scott will bring this man to you. This young man is going to come from the teaching area. But whatever you do, don't go trying to match him up to Scott. Your dad, he's talking again of John. Please, who is John? You've got John around you."

"I don't know a John," I said, almost getting annoyed. *I don't know a John!* She told me to bring flowers to Pat.

"Who is Pat?" she asked.

"Pat is Scott's mother," I replied.

"Well, Scott would like you to bring her flowers on her next birthday." Without missing a beat, she continued. "Who is studying to be a doctor?"

"I am!"

"Don't give it up. He's going to follow you through all the way. You will do wonderful, and he is going to be with you all the way."

Before we ended, she asked if I had any questions for her. I trusted her, so I asked.

"Will there be love in my life again? Did you see me married in the future?" She already had said I would, but I needed to hear the answer again.

"Without a doubt," she shot back without hesitation. "You will be happily married." I was comforted, not just by her words, but by the loving, confident way she said them. They enveloped me like a warm, fleece blanket. To my amazement, she went on. "His name is John, and he is a teacher." *Oh, well.* I felt a twinge of disappointment. I knew I'd have to wait a little longer for this love to enter my life. I didn't know anyone named John with whom I could imagine myself, and I didn't know any teachers.

My ventures into spirituality also got me to thinking about ways I could keep Scott, my father—and myself—alive. I came up with several.

In my father's memory, I planned to learn to cook and not care what others think. In Scott's memory, I planned to not worry or take life too seriously. In both their memories, I planned to enjoy the moment, be silly and goofy, treat others with kindness, exercise, and live each day with spunk, spirit, and humor.

Having those plans allowed me to start letting go and take care of myself.

The bottom line, I realized, is not running away from grief. It has to be faced head-on. It's ugly, scary, and, at times, downright gut-wrenching, feel-like-throwing-up terrifying. I am grateful I had two parents who were never afraid to show their emotions and express love. Their example helped me to heal. I realized I would not feel better if I stuffed my grief.

What I came to understand is that recovery from grief is just as personal as grief itself. No one could help me heal except myself. Friends provided comfort and a listening ear, but *I* had to be willing to seek out that help. Books offered education, guidance, and tools, but *I* had to put those tools into action. The pain would remain unless *I* did something about it and blazed a new trail for love in my life.

By the fall of 1995, Kristen had finished graduate school at the University of Arizona and moved to Red Hook, New York, a quaint, sleepy little town near the Hudson River. Visiting her at her parents' place was such an escape, away from anyone who knew me. I didn't need to worry about looks of pity and sorrow. Her parents had seen me grow up. They were gloriously nutty, the kind of people you don't need to impress. You could say or be anything. So when I visited, I knew I could completely let down my guard.

Kristen and I took long walks around the local high school track, lap after lap after lap. She welcomed the full expression of whatever I was feeling. I was shocked that one friend could tolerate so much, but I suppose my strong emotion was tempered by our laughter and reminiscing about our crazy days of high school and young adulthood. After supper, she and I would continue talking on the patio. Her parents often had to tell us to come inside after midnight. They were afraid that our laughter would wake up the neighbors.

We also spent hours upon hours in nearby Rhinebeck at the Omega Bookshop. I needed to get my hands on any metaphysical, spiritual book that I could—books about near-death experiences, angels, life after death, and your relationship with your loved one after death. On one of my ventures with Kristen there, I just had to find a title by Shakti Gawain that had been recommended to me, *Creative Visualization: Use the Power of Your Imagination to Create What You Want in Your Life*. This book is based on The Law of Attraction, which states, basically, that what we think about and focus on is what we attract into our lives. Creative visualization is one purposeful method of manifesting what we would like in our lives. For it to work, we need to be very clear about what we want, visualize it, and ask for it. I practically devoured the book in the store before bringing it home. It brought me hope.

I came across the book at the perfect time. I'd processed Scott's death as best I could and dated all of the "safe" men. I was ready to live. To me, living meant loving a partner again. Thank God Scott had taught me that was possible. But there was a problem. Having known him, I knew real, unconditional love. I could settle for nothing less, so I had to get serious about what I wanted in a relationship.

Gawain wrote about the Universe responding to energy levels and wanting specifics. The more detailed you can be about listing your desires, she wrote, the easier it is for the Universe to deliver. I carefully prepared for my creative visualization exercise. Along the way, I second-guessed myself, felt crazy, got my hopes up, and then smashed my own hopes. But I did the damn exercise, anyway: I made my list. Since I was looking for a man, I listed all the qualities I wanted in a life partner:

- Intelligent
- Employed
- Sense of humor
- Good looking
- Physically fit
- Loves the outdoors
- Loves children
- Wants at least two children
- Is not intimidated by my intelligence or frustrated by my lack of common sense
- Loves to bike
- Loves to ski

While visiting Kristen, I picked up some incense in nearby Woodstock. I thought I was hip buying incense—and in Woodstock, of all places! I purchased "Nag Champa," a light and airy fragrance of Indian origin. A combination of frangipani (plumeria) and sandalwood, Nag Champa is often used to purify an area, for meditation, and when seeking spiritual enlightenment. It seemed like a great choice for my visualization exercise. Also, Kristen often burned Nag Champa at her house, so the aroma reminded me of the love of her family.

List in hand with incense burning, I sat on the pink carpet of my childhood bedroom and asked the Universe to be kind and deliver this man to me. Over and over, I stated each quality in my mind and out loud.

"Please, Universe. I'm ready. No more gun-toting, pot-smoking, tree-loving, parking lot-peeing characters," I said. "Send me love. I'm ready now."

Then off I went to follow my bliss, skiing and biking in the mountains, which always have held a healing quality for me, just as they did for my father. Those mountains, big enough to contain all my pain and sorrow, saved me spiritually, emotionally, literally.

My father loved to tell me one of his favorite memories of me: I was ten years old and leaned back on the chairlift, my face pointed toward the sun, and said, "This is the life." Yes, it is, and, because my father was a good man, it was for him a good death, granted on his own terms.

It's difficult to explain or understand how landscape can heal. It's just landscape. It doesn't talk to me. It's not giving me advice or a hug. But I still have days when it seems only the mountains understand. That's why I don't mind skiing or biking in the mountains by myself. In fact, there are days that's just what I need.

My buddies on the mountain also provided a kind of support. Skiing and biking were not just sports for me. They were ways of connecting with others. My mountain buddies knew what pain I had been through, and they were rooting for me. When I let them know that I was ready to stop dating men that were wrong for me and find someone who was right for me, my friend Ed gave me a rose quartz nugget. He took it out of his pocket and handed it to me in the middle of the dance floor at the bar at Camelback Mountain while the band Big Orange Cone was playing.

"Here, Peggy," he said. "This is rose quartz. Rose quartz is known as the stone of love. Keep it in your pocket, and it will help attract love. It will help attract the right man to you."

I took it from him and put it in my jeans pocket. The gift was sweet of him and a nice gesture, but I certainly didn't believe that a stone would bring me love. "What the heck," I thought. "I've got nothing to lose!" So I carried that rose quartz nugget in my pocket every day.

About two months later, on May 11, 1996, Helen, a friend I'd met skiing at Camelback in 1993, was hosting a thirtieth birthday party for her boyfriend. All our skiing-and-biking buddies were going. I really didn't want to go, expecting to confront some painful sights: happy couples. While driving up to the Poconos, I thought about Scott a lot. Then I asked, *Scott, if you're here, have something played on the radio that relates to you.* Then I switched stations and out came our wedding song, "I Can See Clearly Now." *That was just coincidence. If it's really you, play another song for me.* The next song was "Blue Sky" by the Allman Brothers. The music transported me to the 1992 concert when Scott told me that the lyrics described how he felt about me. *What does this mean? What is he trying to tell me?*

When I arrived, we all went on a fun-filled, mud-filled mountain bike ride. When we got back to the house, John DeLong was there. I'd never met him, but I'd heard that he was back from Colorado, at least for the summer, and that his engagement was off. I felt bad for him, having some idea what lost love felt like. He stood out at the party because he was the only one not covered in mud—until we all got to take showers.

I came downstairs after my shower, relieved to feel clean and have my hair look decent. I don't know why, but I wanted to impress John. A couple of people told me John had been asking about me while I was in the shower. He asked if I was the girl whose fiancé and father had died. I knew Helen and my sister, Debbie, liked him, but I had some questions of my own. Nursing a beer, I asked some of the other girls: "Is it true he broke off his engagement three months ago? How long is he in town? What is he like?"

Everyone had great things to say about him. We floated toward one another across the room. There was excitement to our conversation, and we talked the entire night. For two people who had just met, we were awfully comfortable together.

At one point, I stood in the front doorway of my friend's house, looking at an approaching storm through the screen. I felt him behind me. The hairs on the back of my neck stood up. He stood behind me and wrapped his arms around me.

"Will you marry me?" he said, teasing. Debbie overheard him and told him he needed her approval, which she gave. We laughed at the absurdity of it all.

John had just purchased a jeep. Outside, he proudly showed it to me. Leaning against it, we had our first kiss as I remembered what that medium had said: I would marry a man named John. But this John wasn't a teacher. She was either only half-right, or this was the wrong John. I wanted her to be half-right. He kissed me so passionately that I felt alive in a way that I hadn't felt since October 11, 1994.

After kissing in his car, we came back to the party where it was obvious to our friends that we'd spent some time alone. I'm not sure how John's face looked, but I know that I could not hide my mischievous grin!

"Don't go home with him," my friend Polly warned. She wanted what was best for me and couldn't see me as a one-night stand. I caught her drift: *don't go home with him, and maybe there will be a next time.* I did not go home with him. He asked me for my phone number and said he'd call.

The next night, John rang the front doorbell of our house. I answered. *So handsome in khakis and a polo shirt*, I thought. *A preppy?* I was excited to ride in his jeep for the first time. I didn't want to go to dinner anywhere in my hometown because I knew too many people. Even if people's eyes conveyed warmth and happiness at my being on a date, I just wanted to be private. I didn't want to drive to Morristown, either, because it was a longer drive. So we chose The Mendham Pub. Even though I'd been there many times, this night felt like the first time. It was the first time—in my new life.

After dinner, John and I went to the playground of my elementary school, Marion T. Bedwell in Bernardsville. The equipment was different, but being there still brought back a familiar childhood feeling. We parked across the street in the parking lot of my town pool, another special place where I'd spent many carefree days in childhood, arriving at 8:00 a.m. for swim team practice and staying all day to swim, bask in the sun, and get paid to braid hair.

John and I walked across the street. We climbed the ladder to the top of the wooden playset, where there was a square, flat, 4' x 4' platform to stand on. We sat down and talked. He began with, "You have sexy calf muscles."

"What?" I asked, surprised.

"Really. They are quite sexy. Muscular. I can imagine all the miles you've ridden on your bike with those muscles." I blushed.

"Well, you could have seen them in action if you got to Pete's party on time!" I reminded him how he missed the mountain bike part of his best friend's party.

"I would love to have been there. Especially to see those legs! But I had to work." *Yay! He has a job! And he sounds responsible. I like that!* He added, "What a bummer. I could have had four more hours with you." *Oh, how charming and flattering he is.*

We sat leaning against the wooden posts, with our legs outstretched, aiming toward the ladder we had just climbed. He put his hand on my knee. Although it was too dark to see clearly, I could tell that he felt my bumpy scar. Rather than pulling his hand away quickly as I feared he might do, he flattened his hand and squeezed my knee. As an avid skier and University of Colorado student of Kinesiology, he knew what that scar meant.

"ACL tear? he asked, already knowing the answer.

"Yep. I took a little spill on the last day skiing in college. Lucky for me, the surgeon was also the surgeon for the United States Ski Team. I was in good hands. But it's still an ugly scar."

"It certainly is not," he said. "You know what they say about scars? They're a sign of strength. Of difficulty overcome." That scar had bothered me still, even though my surgery was six years ago. It was still pink, raised, and bumpy. In my self-consciousness, I tried to take the focus off my knee.

"What surgeries have *you* had?" I asked.

"Too many to count!" he joked.

"Tell me about it." I wanted to know. I wanted to know everything about him.

"Well, I shattered my ankle pretty badly when I was in the service."

"What service?" I asked. *Was he talking about the military?* I had not known anyone my age in the military.

"I was in the United States Air Force for four years. Pararescue." *Wow. Now I'm impressed. While I was drinking beer and skiing when I was not in class at the University of Vermont, he was a young man serving his country.* He continued, "I was honorably discharged after I shattered my ankle. I must have made 100 jumps or so out of aircraft, and my ankle had had enough. It just shattered on impact."

"I can't believe that you were in the Air Force. How selfless. I must say, I'm impressed." He seemed uncomfortable talking about it, quickly changing the subject.

"So this was your elementary school?" he asked.

"Yep! I was here, kindergarten through sixth grade. I loved this school." Pointing to the field ahead in the dark, I said, "And there are the Polo Grounds, where my dad used to take us sledding. And there's the town pool. I was the worst one on the swim team! And there's the pond where we used to ice skate after school in the winter." While seated in one spot, I could point and show him the locations of hundreds of childhood memories.

After talking for a while, we just stared at the stars. The sky was clear, the stars bright. "I love how with the light of the moon, I can see your beautiful face." Again, I blushed and looked down. He put his fingers under my chin and gently lifted it up. Without taking his fingers off my chin, he gently guided my face toward his. Then he kissed me with such passion. I felt hope. I felt excitement. I felt beautiful.

Two days after our first date, John came over again on a sunny, gorgeous Sunday. We hiked at Jockey Hollow in Morristown National Historical Park, where I'd gone in my high school years to run a three-mile loop, often when I experienced emotional pain. Something about those woods comforted me, although they were eerie, too. Many Revolutionary War soldiers, encamped there with General George Washington in the brutal winter of 1779-1780, died in the elements. Such suffering. But the place took on a different comfort for me when I was there with John. We sat on a bridge over a stream and talked. He held my hand the entire time. My wrist tingled as his forefinger delicately brushed against my skin.

Conversation with John was easy. I felt as though we had known each other for years. But I really knew nothing about him! "Where do you want to live after graduate school? I mean, where would you eventually like to settle down?" he asked.

"Anywhere near the mountains. As long as skiing is not too far. I need to be near skiing. Vermont would be really nice! I loved going to college and living in Vermont. Or Colorado. But that would be hard to leave my family."

"I love Colorado," John said. "I'm not sure what I'm going to do." He paused. "I'm supposed to go back there in September. I was coaching the development team at the University of Colorado at Boulder." With each word he uttered, my interest in this handsome man who shared my love for skiing was growing deeper by the minute.

"Are you going to go back?" I asked, afraid of his answer.

"I don't know. You're making that really hard," he said seriously. Then he said what I really wanted to hear. "I've got no commitments. There's really nothing I want to go back for. I can ski anywhere, and I can coach anywhere." I was relieved to hear that he had no intention of trying to work things out with his former fiancée. I *needed* to know that. My heart had been broken through death. I didn't want to knowingly set myself up for my heart to be broken again.

"How can it be that we never met before, with so many friends in common?" he wondered.

"I know!" I exclaimed. "I can't believe that you were racing for Jack

Frost at the same time that I was on the Big Boulder Freestyle Team. My father LOVED Jack Frost, and he kept trying to get us to ski there instead. But we loved Big Boulder. That was tough for him. Four kids against one."

"Who knows?" John said. "Maybe we would have dated in high school! I think you were hanging out with kids from my high school."

We went through some names, and sure enough, John went to high school with some kids on my freestyle team. Even though John and I just met, it was so comforting for me to know that we shared a similar past of skiing in the Pocono Mountains, and we were friends with the same cast of characters!

John stayed for dinner at my house and spent time with my mother—a quiet meal with just the three of us, quite a contrast from the boisterous Sunday night dinners with my father, Scott, my sister, and my sister's husband. It was different, but different was not bad. I loved being with John, and I loved that he spent time with my mother. As she had already moved on after my father's death and was dating Ed, I knew that she was happy (and likely relieved) for me to date again, too, happily knowing her daughter was moving out of grief. It had been almost two years since Scott died.

I could tell that my mother liked John, and that meant a lot to me. Normally a fairly quiet woman, she engaged in conversation and asked John many questions, not in an interrogative way, but in a way that demonstrated that genuine interest in knowing him better. This touched me, but I also found it quite brave of her. We had both lost so much. She was allowing herself to become emotionally connected to a man who was beginning to mean something very special to me.

As the oddball in my family, my mother did not like to ski. She quit after we were all old enough to get on the chairlift by ourselves. She still came with us to the mountain, knitting to keep herself busy, and lovingly warming up our toes with her hands when we came in for a break. But she knew that John loved to ski, and she sensed that this was a way to connect with him.

"So you like to ski, John?" she asked.

"Yes," he replied. "As much as Peggy. Maybe more! I was skiing at Jack Frost when Peggy was skiing at Jack Frost's sister mountain, Big Boulder. Have you ever skied at Jack Frost?"

"Oh, yes, I have!" I couldn't wait to hear what my mother had to say. I had no recollection of her ever skiing at Jack Frost. She continued, "Peggy and I got stuck on a sheet of ice on the headwall of Jane's Lane at Jack Frost when she was about seven years old. That was the last day of skiing for me!"

"Jane's Lane! I know it well," John said. My mother had not skied in over twenty years, and here she was, finding a way to connect with this new man in my life. This meant the world to me. I wondered if the memory was painful for her, as Jack Frost was a very special place for my father. Not only was she connecting with John, but she was connecting with him over a place where my father spent every single Wednesday in the winter for over twenty years. *My mother is one special lady.*

After dinner, John and I went back to the playground in the dark. Once again, we were treated to a clear, inky sky of bright stars that fanned the flame ignited between us two nights earlier. John's kisses brought me back to life. His touch made me feel wanted and desirable, sparking a passion in me that had been dormant for a year and a half.

Still, I couldn't help but think of Scott. At first I felt guilty. Being kissed by this wonderful, handsome man triggered memories of Scott. I told myself that was normal. I told myself it was actually a good sign—a sign that I could feel passion again, something I had questioned and worried about. But I had my answer: I could! The experience taught me it was possible for me to have feelings for another man. Until that moment, those feelings had been only a hope, not a reality.

I didn't see John again until Thursday. He lived an hour away, and I was in the midst of wrapping up the first year of my doctoral program while preparing for comprehensive exams. Starting that Thursday, we saw each other five days in a row. The challenge was finding somewhere private to go. He was staying with his former fiancée's parents, which was weird, and my mother and Ed were always at my house. So John and I went out most of the time, hiking, biking, dining, taking in movies, and going to the playground. But after seeing each other for five days straight, I got spooked. My feelings for him were too strong, too fast. It didn't feel safe. He was someone I could see spending my future with, and that was just so damn scary. I was terrified of having my heart broken again. He was the kind of man I'd asked the Universe to deliver, which terrified me. Since he seemed very right for me, and I felt wonderful being with him, I did what anyone in their right mind would do: I broke up with him.

At a restaurant on a Thursday night I told him I was feeling afraid because things were moving so fast. True. I told him I wanted to feel single and date other people. Not true.

"I understand, Peg," he said. His kindness made me like him even more. *Damn it!* "We'll just be friends. How's that?"

Relief washed over me. I felt safe again.

# The Choice

## Summer 1996

The next morning, John called to ask if we could get together that night.

"I'd love to make you dinner," he said.

"What?" I asked. "Didn't I just break up with you?" He laughed. I did, too. There was nothing to fear. We were just friends.

On Saturday, June 1, 1996, my heart pounded as I drove up to the condo where John was staying. *What the hell am I nervous about? We're just friends.* But those kisses. I could not forget them. I watched him cut up garlic as he prepared our meal.

"I'm using sesame oil," he explained. "It's just the flavor I want." He cut up red pepper and broccoli and tossed the noodles in boiling water as he sautéed the vegetables in the oil. Tantalizing aromas filled the condo.

After the meal, we sat on the balcony and talked for hours, learning more about each other. The moon was full. A summer breeze cooled us. Time passed quickly. "Oh my goodness! It's two o'clock in the morning!" I said, as we headed inside.

"I don't want you driving home this late. You're welcome to stay here," he offered. I didn't want to drive an hour home at that hour either, so I decided to take him up on his offer and stay over. But where should I sleep? On the couch? In his room? Funny, but I didn't feel then that we were just friends.

As if sensing my uncertainty, he said, "I'll sleep on the couch. You can have my bedroom. Let me go upstairs and get some things." *Oh, how sweet and thoughtful. But, hmmm, that's not really what I want.*

I didn't want to be separated from him. It was very clear to me that I wanted to be WITH him. He went upstairs to his bedroom to gather some things for sleeping on the couch. Without any coercion from him, I went to his room while he was still there. "Great," I said. "I'll take your room. But I want you to stay," I added softly. He smiled, then approached me and gave me a long, warm hug. Two nights earlier, I'd felt so unsafe with John because he was so right for me. Being in his arms that night made me feel loved and secure. At last, I was allowing myself to take a chance and live my life.

We awakened early to birdsong. Though we hadn't gotten much sleep, I was energized—not tired. We ate breakfast on the balcony and talked for hours as the sun heated the day. Reluctantly, I left in the early afternoon, needing to study for exams.

That night, he called me to tell me how beautiful and sweet I was.

"I love looking at you," he said, "even when you're sleeping in my arms."

The next few days, I did my best to push John out of my mind so I could concentrate on exams. He drove an hour to see me, giving me a sweet, hour-long study break, only to return home when my studying resumed.

I took my exams on Friday, June 7. John came over afterwards with a rose and took me out to dinner to celebrate.

The next day, we attended a wedding at which I introduced him to all my coworkers, a group that knew Scott well and saw me through every day of his diagnosis, illness, and death. In no time, though, John had everyone at our table laughing. My boss winked at me in approval. John and I slow danced to "Have I Told You Lately (That I Love You)," a Van Morrison song. He pulled me close and quietly sang every word of the song to me. I closed my eyes as tears streamed down my cheeks.

We spent all of June 1996 together when we weren't working. We tested the waters with love language. On June 9, we talked about "falling in love" with each other. The next day, we both said the words, "I love you." On June 10, my world rocked as I remembered, suddenly, John was leaving for Colorado in September. I knew he was going, of course, at least in some part of my mind. *Why was I developing such feelings for him, making him a part of me, meshing our social worlds?* I'd been through this before. But this time, I was the one staying.

It was too late, though. I was in love and, the more John and I knew about one another, the more we felt our love was meant to be. In fact, we were astounded our paths had not crossed sooner since we had many mutual friends from the Poconos. Before one of our dates, we were looking at one of my photo albums from high school.

"What are my friends doing in your photo album?" he asked.

"What do you mean? These are *my* friends!" He pointed to one picture in which I was wearing a competition bib.

"That's 'Boogie in the Bumps' at Big Boulder. I was there that day!" It was also strange that I was on the front cover of the Jack Frost/Big Boulder brochure for the 1982-1983 ski season, and he was on the cover for the 1988-1989 ski season.

Another night, John noticed my father's crazy clown wig in the dining room.

"Hey, what's that?" he asked, looking as if he'd seen it before.

"My dad used to ski in that clown wig," I replied.

"*He* was your father?" John exclaimed. "I knew your father!!"

"He'd wear it on Wednesdays at Jack Frost and on weekends at Big Boulder," I explained. Through one of our previous conversations, we learned that while I was at Big Boulder on weekends, he was at Jack Frost. Since John worked as a ski instructor at Jack Frost, he was there on Wednesdays. Like all the other regulars, he spoke to the man in the clown wig, sharing pleasantries and a few laughs.

I'm very grateful for that silly wig. Without it, I'd never have known that John and my late father had spoken. If not for the wig, they may never have talked at all.

It was strange to spend our first weekend together in the Poconos at my family's camper. When we went out to dinner at a local favorite restaurant, we ran into mutual friends I'd known since I was ten years old. Knowing both our stories of heartache, they were elated to see us together.

As our bond grew ever stronger, John told me that he wanted me to tell him not to return to Colorado. As much as I loved him and wanted him to stay, I told him that I could not do that. Just as Scott did not ask me to stay, I did not want to ask John to stay. I never wanted him to resent me. If he stayed, it would be his decision, 100 percent.

We spent our first summer together going on hikes at the Cross Estates where we chose a perfect dinner spot: a large log over a stream. We ate serenely, listening to the water flow. During the week we had dinner together as often as we could. On weekends we traveled to Vermont and the

Poconos and visited Kristen in Red Hook and Nancy, who had moved to Connecticut.

I knew John had made up his mind about Colorado when he said that we better start looking for apartments before school started and I had no free time. On August 26, we signed a lease on a two-bedroom place in Summit, New Jersey, knowing that some people were scared for us and thought we were moving too quickly, setting ourselves up to get hurt. But we felt right together.

Immediately after moving in, we started getting ready for the Second Annual Scott Unger Memorial Bike Ride to benefit The Valerie Fund, which supports comprehensive health care for children with cancer and blood disorders. At the first bike ride a year earlier, I was single, missing Scott, and still in a lot of pain and grief. I was touched at how many friends, family, and coworkers came to bike and support the event in Scott's memory.

A year later, much had changed. I was looking forward to introducing John to Scott's parents at the event. I felt sick, though, and the autumn air was chilly. We were running late, too, so John quickly grabbed a fleece pullover from our closet and put it on to help keep him warm.

"Umm, you can't wear that," I said bluntly. He had pulled down the bright blue fleece with purple trim that Scott had worn everywhere. It was the only item of Scott's that I had saved. There was no way I could allow John to wear it when he met Scott's parents. They would have recognized it right away as their son's. I didn't even wear it. It just stayed at the top of the closet.

"Why can't I wear it? What's going on?"

I had to tell him.

"John, that was Scott's fleece," I said, "and his parents will recognize it immediately." I know that John understood, but he was hurt that I still had it.

"Are you ever going to let go of him?" he asked, standing near the front door.

"I *have* let him go!" I yelled defensively, still standing in the bedroom.

"No, you haven't. You still have his fleece. Why do you still have his fleece if you've let go of him?" he asked, angrily. I was surprised. I'd never seen John so upset. I didn't know how to answer him. Why *did* I still have Scott's fleece? Tears of sadness and lingering grief streamed down my face.

"I don't know," I muttered. Clearly, my response was no comfort to John. I didn't blame him for being upset. As much as I loved him, I was still trying to make sense of my own emotions. It had only been two years since Scott's passing. I was in the strangest state, still grieving his loss while I knew I truly loved John. My feelings didn't make sense to me, so I didn't even attempt to explain them to John.

"Am I ever going to come first?" he asked, walking toward me in the bedroom.

"This is not about coming first! He's dead! You're first!" That was not the way I wanted to convey my feelings for John. "I mean, *you* are the one I am with. *You* are the one I love. *You* are the one I want to spend my life with." I cried, sitting on the edge of our bed. John came closer and sat next to me. He cried, too.

"I sometimes feel I can never live up to Scott's memory," he said. "I can never live up to his ghost." To hear those words made me sad. *Is that the way I make him feel? What am I doing wrong that he cannot sense how much I love him and that he is first?* I was disappointed in myself for not heeding the warning Scott had sent me through the medium: I was putting him on a pedestal that no man could ever live up to.

"And I don't understand why you're so nervous about me meeting his parents," John continued. "That upsets me!"

"I'm nervous because I love you. I want a future with you, and I want their blessing!" Unfortunately, we had to put the conversation on hold because we were late for the bike ride. Still sitting on the bed, we held each other. We then stood up. John took off the fleece. Gently, he folded it and placed it at the edge of the bed.

When we arrived at the Chatham train station, the site of the event, there were two hundred people there, so John and I didn't have a chance to even look at each other, much less discuss anything. In the parking lot, people were removing their bikes from racks, adjusting helmets, filling water bottles, and catching up. To my surprise, I saw Kevin, Scott's roommate from the hospital during his first chemotherapy treatment. "Kevin, I'm so happy you're here. You were such an inspiration to Scott. Thank you for coming."

"Wouldn't miss it," Kevin said, adjusting his helmet over his head while winking at me. His hair had grown back, and he looked wonderful, healthy, and handsome. I was happy for him. It took every ounce of energy within me to hold back my tears. He survived! Soon everyone went to the starting area where they received a map. As this was not a race, bikers took off at their own pace.

John and I did the ride with different people. I felt relieved he was riding with people he knew well. That ride was about Scott. Yet I could not wait to get home and talk to John about the relationship between the two of us.

I believe in soul mates. What I did not believe was that I'd be blessed enough to have two. After losing Scott, I was convinced beyond a doubt

I'd be single for the rest of my life. After experiencing that level of love, I knew I couldn't settle for anything less, but I also knew I didn't want to be alone. I had too much love in me not to share it with someone.

I also knew any man I dated after Scott had to trust that he could make me happy in spite of everything I'd been through. He had to be a man of compassion, depth, courage, strength, and bravery. I believe it takes these qualities to be with a young widow. John had them all. I understood how he was feeling. Really, I did. How could anyone possibly live up to a deceased partner? One who was treasured by so many? I was touched that John had the courage to even ask me out, let alone allow himself to fall in love with me. I had always felt that just because of this alone, he was one very special man.

Finally, the race ended, and we went back to the apartment to finish our conversation. We sat on the couch in our small living room, feet touching, facing each other. John was still seeking an answer about why I had the fleece. I tried to explain that I did not understand it myself. Even I grew frustrated with the effort.

"See!" I said. "This is what I mean about me having too much baggage. Sometimes I wonder why you would even want to be with me! Why do you want to be with me? It's too complicated. I'm too complicated."

"I know you've been through so much, and I know that you love me," he said. "It just hurts that you have held on to something of his and that you brought it here. It just makes me wonder whether or not your heart will ever be 100 percent for me."

"But it already is 100 percent for you," I said. "I love you. You are the one I want to spend the rest of my life with. When someone dies, love for that person does not die. Scott will always be a part of me. Part of the reason I am with you is because I thought you understood that. If you died, a part of you would always be with me. My love for Scott is in the past and part of me, but it is different from the love I have for you now. Our love makes me feel alive. You make me feel alive again." Instead of appearing comforted, John seemed confused and hurt. He asked an even bigger question.

"Then why are you still wearing the engagement ring he gave you?" *Of course, the ring! I hadn't realized the impact that still wearing my engagement ring had on John. Stupid me! Why hadn't I taken it off?* I knew the reason: I had not been ready to part with it. Not until that very moment when I realized I absolutely needed to show John my heart belonged to him.

"Sweetheart," I told him. "I have something to show you." I went into the bedroom and picked up the blue fleece that was still neatly folded where John had placed it. I put the fleece in a bag to be donated or given to someone who loved Scott. "Now watch what I'm going to do next very carefully." I wiggled the engagement ring off my finger and placed it in my jewelry box. "I'm never wearing it again. I'm going to give it to Scott's mother."

I was scared of the symbolic meaning of taking off the ring for good, but I had to let go of Scott. To me, relinquishing the ring meant I was saying good-bye to Scott in the physical world and choosing to give 100 percent of myself to John. Frankly, when I made this decision, I felt as if I was betraying Scott, but then I remembered my dad's words: "I know Scott would not want you to be sad." I remembered the first medium's words that Scott would be ready to let me go after the first anniversary of his death. I remembered the second medium's words that I would be ready to let Scott go after the second anniversary of his passing, which was right then. I couldn't believe the timing.

Deciding to take off Scott's engagement ring was one of the most emotionally difficult things I've ever done, but it was necessary. There wasn't room for both of my soul mates in the physical world. I wish John had told me before how he felt about me wearing the ring. But duh! I should have known better. I felt bad for making John feel second best for so long. Whenever I had that ring on my finger, it was as if a part of Scott was always in the room with us. That little girl at the preschool who told me that the ring was "powerful" was right.

As time went on, my get-togethers with Scott's mother became less frequent, but they were still quite in the ordinary routine. It wasn't unusual that I called her to get together for dinner. Not knowing the surprise I had in store, she gladly accepted my invitation.

After we ordered at the restaurant, I took the ring out of my purse and handed it to her. Even though it was in a box, she immediately knew what it was. She held the box in her hand and cried. When she opened it, we both cried. I needed her to have the ring, though. The diamond came from Scott's father's mother. After she died, Scott was told he could have the diamond to put in an engagement ring for his future wife. It didn't feel right to pass the ring down to one of my family members, or to my future children, if I ever had any. I also knew that if I did not keep it myself, Scott would want me to return it to his family.

"This means the world to me, dear," his mother said. We both sobbed. I never realized before that day how powerful the release would be when I gave up that special piece of jewelry.

That Thanksgiving I worried how I'd feel since it was the week of the anniversaries of my father's death, wake, and funeral. But I saw evidence that we were all beginning to heal. My father's clown wig remained in the dining room, and we felt his presence. As we sat around the table, we all stated something for which we were thankful. I was nervous when it got to John's turn. *What would he say?* John looked a bit uneasy. He cleared his throat.

"I'm thankful to be a part of a wonderful family," he said. We thought he was done, but he wasn't. "I'm thankful to be with a woman I love and care so much about." My heart melted.

In the months that followed, John and I talked about marriage. We knew we wanted to spend the rest of our lives together. Still, we needed more time. Yet I wondered every day, *Is today the day? Is he going to ask me to marry him?* I knew we were getting close when John told me he prayed to my father in heaven and asked for his blessing to marry me. While he was having celestial conversations, he also told Scott he would always be good to me and take care of me.

I did not want to pick out my ring, but John wanted a general idea of what kind I liked. As we walked along the main street of our quaint town of Madison, lined with boutiques, I showed him a ring I liked in the window of a jewelry store. Passing that window was part of my almost daily running route. Each time I went by, I'd gaze down at the ring and think about my future with John. One day, the ring was gone! I gasped.

# I Can See Clearly Now

Not too long after that, John and I planned a trip to Vermont to hike at Sunset Rock. One day we packed a lunch, planning to sit on the rock and enjoy the view, each other's company, and a bite to eat. The sky looked clear. We could see for miles, to infinity. Everything shone an emerald green. John seemed to be acting a bit strange. At one point he leaned over and kissed me. Then he did it again, the second time reaching into his backpack, taking out the ring box, and opening it to reveal the beautiful ring.

"Would you like to spend the rest of your life with me and be my wife?" I could not stop crying. I wanted to shout, "Yes!" But all I could do was nod my head as tears streamed down my face. It was the fairy-tale proposal I'd always dreamed of. I wanted to shout the news to the world. Instead, I told the clerk at the check-out counter at the small gas station convenience store where we stopped on our way back to the bed and breakfast.

"I'm engaged! I'm getting married!" I said, as I handed over money to buy my first bridal magazine.

The months that followed were bittersweet. For the second time, I was excited to be getting married. But I had lost Scott and I couldn't shake either my fear of losing John or my sadness that my father would not walk me down the aisle. Those feelings haunted me during every wedding-related appointment.

I tried to minimize the fear by making the wedding plans different so that my experiences would not bring back memories of Scott. Of course,

I chose a different bridal shop. I would never have gone back to the shop that made my friends pay for their bridesmaid dresses, took my friend to small claims court, and told me that my gown would be used as a sample! I sought a shop located in a different direction so that even the traveling and landmarks would not trigger my fear of loss.

Purposefully, I chose other different details. A different venue. Instead of a DJ, a band. Instead of a winter wedding, a summer wedding.

Despite my efforts to fight my fear, the more I loved John each day, the more I feared losing him. At the time John and I were planning our wedding, it had only been three years since Scott's passing. Although my heart belonged to another man, I still had vivid memories and even a visceral reaction with some memories related to this loss. If I let my mind wander too much, I could even experience the nausea that came with profound loss. The only difference: I was not losing John. It was only a fear.

Nevertheless, the feeling overwhelmed me. I didn't want it to take away my joy as we planned our wedding. During my last engagement, my joy was taken away by something out of my control—Scott's diagnosis of cancer. This time, I had control, and I was determined not to let anything interfere with what was supposed to be one of the happiest times of my life. So I sought professional help with a trusted psychologist. As a budding psychologist myself, I knew the value of psychotherapy. I was grateful for the opportunity to process my feelings in a supportive environment so that they interfered less with my life outside the therapy room.

I'd made great progress in grieving my father's death but getting engaged made me regress and miss my father more. I didn't want my sadness to be stronger than my joy on my wedding day, and I didn't know what to do.

Then a friend gave me a helpful suggestion: she said John and I could go to a place that was special for my father and say our vows there in a ceremony just for him. We decided on Tripod Rock in Kinnelon. We wrote our vows on a small piece of paper, folded the paper, and tucked it safely in the backpack. We decided to make a day of it, so we packed sandwiches, too.

On the way up to the spot, my heart was pounding and not only from the steep climb. I was nervous about what we were about to do.

Halfway up the hill to Tripod Rock, there is a clearing, with a magnificent view from a large, flat rock. Since we were both nervous, we decided that it was best to say our vows first and then eat lunch on the rock. John took off the backpack, took out the paper, and unfolded it. As we hugged, a gentle rain fell, which was odd for such a sunny day. The rain was ever so light. Though we felt the drops on our skin, we did not feel wet. I found them soothing. There was no need to cover ourselves. John said his vows first.

"I, John, take you, Peggy, to be my wife. I promise to be true to you in good times and in bad, in sickness and in health. I will love you and honor you, all the days of my life." He then passed the piece of paper to me, and quietly, I read the same vows to him.

We felt my dad's presence. As John tucked the paper into his backpack, the rain stopped. We believed those drops were my father's tears of joy, falling gently from heaven.

Having that separate ceremony allowed me to focus on what I wanted for my wedding day rather than being sad about what was missing and what I could not have.

On July 31, 1998, the eve of the wedding, my girlfriends had slept over at my childhood home. We woke up the next day, had breakfast, and then dangled our feet in the swimming pool. I felt nothing but joy and gratitude. I had lost so much. Yet so much had been given back to me. I had love again, and I was marrying John in a few hours.

Our wedding was everything I dreamed it would be and more. The day was gorgeous—75 degrees with low humidity, an especially pleasant day for summertime in New Jersey. I basked in every moment of the beautiful ceremony. My brothers walked me down the aisle. My Uncle Wayne played the piano, while my Aunt Harriet and cousins Kathy and Carol sang "Ave Maria" and Barbra Streisand's "Evergreen." I was grateful to stand up there holding hands with such a brave man.

Off we went to the reception at Lenfell Hall in The Mansion, a one hundred-room estate on the campus of Fairleigh Dickinson University in Madison, a historic treasure. The interior staircases and fireplaces are made of Italian marble, the labor of Italian craftsmen. They held cocktail hour on the stone veranda, which overlooked the ornate gardens.

As the guests came inside for dinner, Uncle Wayne blessed the food. Kristen, a poet, gave the toast:

> . . . there is no more qualified example of hope than Peggy, who, with dignity and extraordinary resilience, has shown us what it means to overcome great pain, to find the courage and purpose to rebuild her life.
>
> John, you are a large part of that purpose and something of a hero. Besides a shared passion for the outdoors, sense of humor, and lust for life, the most remarkable aspect of your union with Peggy is that you unwittingly skied the same mountain since

childhood, not knowing that each trip down the slope, each turn or mogul negotiated, was bringing you closer to each other.

It had to have been fate that put you, finally, in Peggy's path that day she arrived at a mutual friend's house covered in mud from a rigorous bike ride. As an avid mountain biker, you knew you met your match. But what foresight to have seen that this mud-covered diamond-in-the-rough would eventually shine. It is because of you now that she shines all the brighter. It is because of your love for each other that this day is filled with promise for us all.

Everyone gave Kristen a long, loud standing ovation. Her toast even earned her a job offer at a major advertising agency in New York City that evening.

The entire day was filled with love. If anything went wrong, I didn't notice. John was perfect. Our wedding day and evening with friends and family was perfect, and our wedding night alone, just the two of us, was perfect.

Then came the honeymoon: three weeks skiing, jetboating, and parapenting in New Zealand. Another love story had begun.

# Epilogue

As the years went on, John and I had three children—two daughters and a son. I completed my doctorate in psychology, and, as fate would have it, John changed fields, leaving kinesiology behind for teaching. Just as the medium predicted, I married a teacher named John.

My wish, my hope, had come true. I found love again. It made me wonder about the creative visualization exercise that I performed in my childhood bedroom when I visualized my ideal partner and asked the Universe to deliver. Curiosity took hold, and I searched for the piece of paper in my notebook where I wrote down all the characteristics I wanted in a partner.

Delighted when I found the list, I was also astonished that John not only met the requirements, but surpassed them:

- Intelligent – He has two master's degrees and blows me away with his intelligence. My mother always jokes that she does not need Google because she has John.

- Employed – He has always been employed since the day we met. In fact, he usually has two jobs at any given time.

- Sense of humor – He makes me laugh every day, and he makes our children laugh.

- Good looking – He caught my eye at that mountain biking party right away.

- Physically fit – All of his sports keep him in shape.
- Loves the outdoors – Every vacation we have had is spent outdoors skiing, hiking, biking, and boating.
- Loves children – He is an elementary school teacher, camp leader, and coach.
- Wants at least two children – We have three.
- Is not intimidated by my intelligence or frustrated by my lack of common sense – Well, maybe a little frustrated by my lack of common sense.
- Loves to bike – We met at a mountain biking party.
- Loves to ski – He is the Head Coach of our children's ski race team.

Day by day, I have learned to live in communion with all my loves on both sides of the veil. I'm always scanning this world for signs from beyond. My father is good at manifesting them, especially in the place he most loved: Jack Frost Mountain.

When Morgan, my middle child, was three years old, I took her out of preschool on a Wednesday to put her in a group lesson at Jack Frost. I knew it would become a private lesson since hardly anyone comes during the week. As we walked through the heavy glass doors and toward our seats in the empty lodge, it was 8:30 a.m.

"Is that man your father?" Morgan asked me in the sweetest voice.

There was no man in sight. I was stunned because my daughter knew my father had passed away. What she didn't know was that before he died, he skied at Jack Frost every Wednesday without fail, regardless of the weather. We were there at just the time he'd be booting up before heading out for first chair and exiting the lodge through the very same doors we'd just come in. Goosebumps.

On my birthday in 2012, we were blessed with about two feet of snow overnight. I was anxious to get to Jack Frost, as the skiing was unusually amazing for the Poconos. It was a Tuesday. My children were off from school for the Presidents' Day holiday, and they were all taking too long to get ready. John agreed to stay back and help them, allowing me to drive to the mountain and get to my birthday present—all that snow!

I couldn't help but think of my father who loved to ski there during the week when there were no crowds, and he could have the place to himself. He could do his lazy zigzagging across the slope without worrying about being hit from behind. I remember his excitement when Jack Frost expanded, opening up East Mountain.

So there I was, skiing that very mountain. The snow and dangerous travel had kept many people away. I skied by myself. Then I got my real gift while riding in the chairlift, looking at my skis. Usually, I don't look down because I'm afraid of heights. I never look up, either because it makes me dizzy. I'm afraid I'll fall off this metal chair dangling from a wire. But that day something made me look straight up.

Flying above me was a bald eagle. He stayed with me, soaring above my head for the entire eight-minute ride. I remembered what Shirley told me: Some say the eagle is a sign the spirit of a loved one is near. On his favorite chairlift and on my birthday, my father blessed me with his presence.

In that moment of seeing the eagle, I felt a sign that the spirit of a loved one was near. Riding on my father's favorite chairlift on my birthday I realized I had survived! I had survived the deaths of the two most important men in my life, just six weeks apart from each other. I felt an overwhelming sense of peace, of comfort, of knowing in my heart that everything is going to be OK, that we are all going to be OK. Life does not end after this life. I will always feel connected to my deceased loved ones. They will find ways to connect with me, and I will *feel* their presence, without a doubt.

With my father, this connection has been through eagle sightings at Jack Frost, his favorite place to ski, and Brady's Lake, his favorite place to go boating and fishing. With Scott, it happens when I hear our wedding song, "I Can See Clearly Now," which became his funeral song. This song has been played on the radio on the anniversary of his death for the past twenty-four years without fail, as well as at other meaningful times, such as making that turn onto the Pacific Coast Highway, the only part we had planned of our honeymoon. But most of all, I've been given the greatest gift of true knowledge and understanding: love never dies.

# About the Author

Dr. Peggy DeLong is a clinical and forensic psychologist who was raised in bucolic Bernardsville, New Jersey. She has a private practice in Long Valley, New Jersey, where she serves as an expert witness, specializing in parenting and child protection issues. Through her private practice and public speaking, Peggy assists individuals and groups to foster gratitude and cultivate joy in everyday living. She also owns Peggy's Midnight Creations, where she designs inspirational, mental health bracelets for life's transitions and challenges.

Dr. DeLong also coordinates a weekly, year-round women's walking group, where she combines her passions for bringing people together with being out in nature and helping individuals improve their mental health. An accomplished psychologist, entrepreneur, speaker, and author, Dr. DeLong feels passionate about connecting with others and helping them live their very best lives, even on the worst of days.

When she's not focused on her businesses, you'll find Peggy with her husband and three children in the mountains, downhill or telemark skiing, kayaking, hiking, or mountain biking.

Find out more about Peggy's services and her bracelets by visiting http://drpeggydelong.com.

Made in the
USA
Lexington, KY